GUESSES

GUESSES
GOOFS
&
PROPHETIC
FAILURES

WHAT TO THINK WHEN
THE WORLD DOESN'T END

JESSICA TINKLENBERG DEVEGA

THOMAS NELSON
Since 1798

NASHVILLE   DALLAS   MEXICO CITY   RIO DE JANEIRO

Published in Nashville, Tennessee, by Thomas Nelson. Thomas Nelson is a registered trademark of Thomas Nelson, Inc.

Page design: Crosslin Creative
Images: Dover Pictorial Archives

Thomas Nelson, Inc., titles may be purchased in bulk for educational, business, fund-raising, or sales promotional use. For information, please e-mail SpecialMarkets@ThomasNelson.com.

ISBN: 9-781-4016-7682-7

Printed in the United States of America

12 13 14 15 16 QG 6 5 4 3 2 1

CONTENTS

FOREWORD

This book comes out of three great loves of my life: the Bible, popular culture, and my students. As a biblical scholar, I know how much the Bible's ancient stories and images continue to have an impact on the modern world. They pop up continually in discussions with my students; I see them in popular media like *True Blood*, and I hear them in music from Leonard Cohen to Kanye West. And yet, I also know how often people who claim to "know" the Bible actually know the traditions passed down to them from their parents, Sunday school teachers, and popular culture. These traditions are not bad; indeed, they are often beautiful and tenderly shared. Unfortunately, they are also often inaccurate, poorly interpreted, or flat out not part of the shared text. Too often, what we think is "in the Bible" is actually an indicator of our own biases and preconceptions, rather than accurate to Scripture, and it leads to stereotyping and mistreatment of others who have a "different Bible" than we do.

In the spring of 2009, I facilitated a senior seminar with my students on apocalyptic texts; in the spring of 2011, a different group of seniors explored death and immortality in the ancient world. In both cases, I learned an enormous amount from my students about the questions they have, and their search to understand the world around them. I hope that this book will be a way for my students to engage biblical texts and their subsequent interpretations with honesty and optimism. I hope it will offer them a path to see others, some of whom are very different, as shared pilgrims on the path to understanding. And I hope that you, the reader, whoever you are, will feel invited to challenge your own perceptions, beliefs, and ideas as you join us on this journey.

The process of writing a book is not a solo endeavor, and I am grateful for those that believed in me and aided me throughout: my editor and fellow sci-fi geek Heather; the Morningside College writing group; my colleagues and dear friends Jeremy, David, Chris, Rachel, Kim, Brenda, and Bruce who acted as cheerleaders and coaches; and my girls, who put up with many lost hours of mom time so I could finish. Thank you all.

INTRODUCTION

★ THIS IS THE END!

The first time I remember hearing about the end of the world, I was at a friend's middle school youth group meeting. That night a member of the senior high group asked me, in serious tones, if I was pre-tribulationist or post-tribulationist. I had never heard either of these words, and I told him so. In an obviously well-rehearsed speech, he told me how the Revelation predicted that the world would end soon and that Christians who were "concerned" about this event were divided as to whether the true believers would be raptured before the earth's devastation or after a period of waiting and testing. He ended his discussion with a pointed reminder that, whatever the correct interpretation of Revelation was, we were going to see the cataclysmic destruction of the world any day now, and that I best be ready for the end. I did not sleep that night.

I never did ask him why it mattered if I was "pre-trib" or "post-trib." I was too scared by the idea that the world was in such bad shape and headed for something worse. I had been a bright-eyed optimist about the world until this point. I was well-fed and had loving parents, brothers who playfully teased me, education, and safety. I thought people were basically good, and thus the world was basically good. Further, it had never occurred to me that the Bible "predicted" anything.

I was raised in the church—for a while my dad was my minister—but in all that time the Bible was understood as a life-guide, a teaching tool, a moral example, and a view into the foundations of our faith. It was not a crystal ball. This young man's view of the world, and of the Bible, was a terrifying new view of everything I thought I understood.

This book is an attempt to understand such interpretations of impending doom, which we generally call *apocalyptic*. Apocalypticism is a belief in the coming end of this (evil) world and the dawn of a new, better one. It comes out of an ancient worldview, borne from feelings of persecution, fear, and distress, held by Jews and the earliest Christians. Because of their common concerns, and shared worldview, the Jews and early Christians produced texts that had many features in common. They relied on similar use of imagery, coded language, and other conventions, and these shared features eventually marked the genre as *apocalyptic*. Some texts like Daniel and Revelation are now part of Scripture, but others such as Enoch did not make the cut. Over centuries, these texts of apocalypticism were reused, reinterpreted, and rediscovered by others, and made to apply to their own time. Eventually, the apocalyptic worldview became widely accepted and much believed. Today, according to some recent surveys, one in four Americans believe that the world will end within his or her lifetime (Keller 8). Many more believe that the end will occur soon, if only slightly after their time on earth is done. What is the draw of such a worldview and where does it come from? How has it appeared and reappeared throughout history, and why do we keep coming back to it? What happens to believers when the end does not arrive on schedule? Since I was that middle school youth, these questions have perplexed me. Perhaps they perplex you too.

THE SCOPE OF THE BOOK

I am a biblical scholar by training. I look at the ancient texts that came to be accepted by Jewish and Christian leaders as authoritative, as well as those they rejected, to understand the mindset of at least some of the founders of these Western faiths. In this book, I will rely on that training for the first part of our discussion, What Is Apocalypticism? The Bible and other ancient Jewish and Christian writings are of a variety of genres and types, including poetry, law, letters, and parables. The genre commonly known as *apocalyptic*, which was mentioned above, is the particular type of literature from which many later prophets of the end have drawn their predictions. In this first section, I will discuss where apocalyptic literature came from as well as what attributes mark it as different from other types of biblical literature. I will then look at specific examples of ancient apocalyptic texts, from the non-biblical book of Enoch to the last book of the Christian New Testament, the Revelation (or the Apocalypse of John as it was known in the ancient world).

Of course, the amazing thing about these ancient texts is that they did not cease to be meaningful after the Canon was closed.

A canon is a collection of authoritative scriptures for the people of a religion. For all Christians, the Canon includes 66 books, 39 in the Old Testament and 27 in the New Testament. Some Christians, such as those of Roman Catholic and Orthodox traditions, also include other books in their canon.

Instead, they informed and were reinterpreted by later Jews and Christians for their own times. In the second section of this book, called When Is the Date of the End? I discuss sixteen such reinterpretations over the past two thousand years. Alas, despite the fact that this is a book on biblical prophecies and popular culture I can't use the very biblical numbers seven or twelve, or even 144,000. Instead the sixteen here have very intriguing features I think you will find interesting. What these sixteen interpretations have in common is that, in each case, the believers thought that they could pinpoint a year, or perhaps even a day, that the end of the world would arrive, based on their own interpretation of the texts. I chose those failed apocalypses because they are specific, use

PRIMARY SOURCES ARE ALWAYS THE WRITINGS CLOSEST TO THE GROUP WE ARE STUDYING. IN BIBLICAL STUDIES, THEY ARE THE BOOKS OF THE BIBLE, BUT WHEN WE STUDY OTHER GROUPS, THE PRIMARY TEXTS MIGHT BE THEIR OWN LETTERS, OR VIDEOS, OR DIARY ENTRIES. THESE ARE DIFFERENT FROM SECONDARY SOURCES, WHICH ARE USUALLY SOMEONE ELSE'S ANALYSIS OF THE PRIMARY SOURCE.

concepts from the textual history of Jews and Christians, and represent a wide range of beliefs about the end. In no way are these examples a complete list of end-times predictions, however. They are presented in chronological order, from shortly after the last book of the New Testament was written up through recent events. For each prediction, I offer a brief history of the prophet's or community's beliefs, the events that led to the forecast, and the aftermath of the failed guess.

In the final section of the book, called When the World Doesn't End, I consider some of the reasons apocalypticism has held on so long when each and every prediction has ultimately failed. I contemplate some psychological, sociological, and theological reasons that people can both weather apocalyptic failure and buy into the next prediction to come down the pike. What is particularly interesting is how people rationalize failure and reorient themselves in order to maintain their beliefs in the face of their prophet's goof. Finally, I will offer you suggestions for approaching the next apocalyptic forecast you hear with faith, optimism, and critical thought.

A FEW SUGGESTIONS FOR ENJOYING THE END OF THE WORLD (IN THIS BOOK)

Throughout the book I attempted to be thoughtful and generous, while not compromising having an accurate and rigorous discussion. This can be hard, and you might at times disagree with me and believe that I have failed. It is my belief that in order to understand where we are today with regard to prophetic movements we must discuss and understand apocalypticism and the biblical literature it grew out of; however, this is not an academic book. I am not explaining the sociology of apocalyptic sects, and I am not going to provide an in-depth commentary on each of the ancient texts. What I want us to focus on here is how we can understand people like the young man I met at youth group that night. In my effort to do so, I have drawn together a diversity of primary sources, scholarly insights, and nontraditional perspectives.

EISEGESIS IS THE ACT OF PUTTING YOUR OWN PRECONCEIVED MEANINGS INTO SCRIPTURE, RATHER THAN DRAWING MEANING OUT. I OFTEN TELL MY STUDENTS THAT EISEGESIS IS A BIBLICAL STUDIES CURSE WORD.

In each case I try to be optimistic that we really can understand and empathize with others. I take my cues from a scholar of religion named J. Z. Smith. He is famous for his study of apocalyptic movements. He once said that as we study religion we must always remember that "nothing human is foreign to me."

There are several types of logic. We can look at the logic of the predictions themselves even if it is only internal to the group or prophet. But we can't stop there. We must also examine how that group's or prophet's logic makes sense as it relates to the history of apocalypticism and its key texts. To do that and understand the people who followed each prophet, we need to use the language of the believers. I will quote extensively in some cases, so that the believers might speak to you in their own words about that which they were or are so very passionate. If you are inclined to be skeptical of apocalypticism, it may strike you from time to time that I am being too generous in my description of the followers or their claims. When you feel that way, remember that the people who believe things you consider crazy are still people. I encourage you to take those people seriously because their beliefs are just as important to them as your beliefs are to you.

However, taking them seriously does not mean that I will never be critical of an apocalyptic group or its ideas in the course of this book. There are times when millennial beliefs are violent, promote hate, or encourage blind obedience. Even groups that don't resort to such over-the-top destructive behaviors can hurt adherents with their demands of time or money. Given my background as a biblical scholar, I tend to be particularly attuned to sketchy use of ancient texts, something we call *eisegesis*.

Beliefs and behaviors like these deserve to be looked at with a certain degree of suspicion, since they clearly can—and have—caused irrevocable harm. You may find that you hold some of these (or similar) potentially dangerous beliefs. The critique of them here might strike you as threatening or blasphemous to your faith. If so, I invite you to consider carefully why the critiques have been leveled, and whether the "threat" to your belief might instead be a new way of thinking that might spare you from even greater harm. I didn't write this book to destroy the faith of others. Instead, the purpose of this book is to understand what we believe, why we each believe it, and how we can understand each other.

Whatever your perspective on the end of time, I hope you will be intrigued by the diversity and intensity of prophetic beliefs. In this short book I look at an incredible array of ideas about the end of time that can involve political figures, agendas and beliefs of groups, or views of society's failures. Sometimes a group's interpretation relies on mathematics, mysticism, or the founder's charisma. There are apocalypses that rely on angels, and some that rely on UFOs. The sheer multitude and broad scope of examples here (and in the many, many more I could not cover) indicate a deep and consistent desire among people for hope, improvement, salvation, and change. As you look at the examples offered from the book of Daniel to the Maya apocalypse of 2012, I hope you will recognize this as well. Whether you are apocalyptic or not, these are desires we all share.

PART 1

WHAT IS APOCALYPTICISM?

★

Apocalypticism is a very old way of thinking. While there is debate regarding the origins of beliefs in the end of the world, there is no doubt that long ago people considered the possibility that someday their known world would end, be replaced, or be renewed. However, to really understand the mindset that led ancient Jewish and Christian writers to imagine an apocalyptic event, we have to start well before even our oldest apocalyptic texts. In fact, we have to start with a different worldview entirely: the wisdom traditions that apocalypticism grew out of.

From wisdom literature, we will turn to a discussion of apocalyptic literature as a genre, including its key features and concerns. As exhausting as all that may sound, we won't be done there. We will dig deeper into biblical and non-biblical apocalyptic writings whose specific ideas continued to influence later thinking.

Genre means the type or kind of writing a piece of literature is. As we know, different writing serves different purposes, and the genre reflects the purpose. For example, a Shakespearean sonnet is not the same as my shopping list. One type of writing—of the genre *poetry*—is meant to evoke strong feelings of beauty or love. The other—of the genre *list*—is intended to convey needed information in the most efficient way possible. The Bible has genres of literature, too, including law, prophetic oracle, letter, apocalyptic, and gospel, just to name a few.

THE WISDOM TRADITION

Wisdom literature, and the worldview behind it, was one direct precursor to the apocalyptic literature we wish to understand. Wisdom traditions were very important within the Jewish and Christian Scriptures as a way of understanding the world and why bad things happen. Apocalyptic traditions that grew out of wisdom literature attempted to answer some of the same questions.

Wisdom traditions in ancient Israel are very old. And some scholars believe that traditions date as far back as the reign of kings Saul, David, and Solomon. However, the existing texts we have (Proverbs, Job, Ecclesiastes, some of the Psalms, Song of Songs, Ben Sira and Wisdom of Solomon) have a long compositional history which likely reaches into the period of the exile of the Judahites by the Babylonians (586 BCE and later). The book of Deuteronomy includes a system of blessings and curses based on a person's actions (Deut. 30), so the wisdom tradition and its almost universal basic view that good things happen to the righteous and bad to the evil are a natural extension of the laws in the Pentateuch. Indeed wisdom literature, as we now understand it, took the idea of reward and punishment in this life to its logical extreme, creating both a unified worldview and an ultimate backlash.

In order to understand the growth of apocalyptic traditions we have to first understand what the concept of *wisdom* implied. Put succinctly, wisdom is the orderly worldview of the sages of Israel and Judah, in which actions resulted in a this-worldly reward or punishment based on the standards of the Law and right action. Consider the following, from Proverbs 28:4, 5, 7, 9:

> Those who forsake the law praise the wicked,
>> but those who keep the law struggle against them.
> The evil do not understand justice,
>> but those who seek the Lord understand it completely. . . .
> Those who keep the law are wise children,
>> but companions of gluttons shame their parents.
> . . . When one will not listen to the law,
>> even one's prayers are an abomination.

Here we see the first of several features that exemplify the Wisdom worldview—humans ought to live according to the standard of the Law. Scholars do not agree about what exactly the sage meant by *law*, but we can guess that it was not too different from the Torah commands that we see in the Scripture today: circumcision as a sign of the covenant, the worship of one God, kashrut (proper behavior in such matters as what to eat), interpersonal justice, and the keeping of holy days. (See for example Wisd. Sol. 6:4; Sirach 24:23; 35:1.) Whatever the specific content of the Law, however, it is clear from the sage's advice that keeping the law was critical to a life of wisdom and justice.

Added to this standard of the Law, the sages often relied on experience to convince their audience that this pursuit of wisdom was prudent. In some forms of the wisdom tradition the self-guided quest for wisdom can even completely replace the standard of the Law. In Ecclesiastes (called Qoheleth) for example, the teacher applied his "mind to seek and to search out by wisdom all that is done under heaven" (1:13) and made a test of various lifestyles to consider their role in the cosmic order (2:1–8). The author of Ben Sira exhorts his reader, "When you gain friends, gain them through testing, and do not trust them hastily" (5:7). Behind this experiential model of gaining wisdom is likely a sense that wisdom is built into the cosmos, that it is "set up, at the first, before the beginning of the earth" (Prov. 8:23). Thus, wisdom can be seen and understood in all the created order, even apart from knowledge of the Law.

From the standard of the Law, and the ordered and pre-dictable nature of the cosmos as a whole, the wisdom tradition draws its second key feature: a strict division between the righ-teous and the wicked. Good people do good things ("keep the Law" or "seek the Lord"), and the bad do bad things ("forsake the Law," etc.). In most wisdom literature humans seldom have mixed motives. Instead, humanity is neatly organized into those who seek wisdom, and those who do not. The division is so orderly that it can be described in poetic couplets.

A third feature of the wisdom worldview, as evident in Proverbs 28:4–9, is the immediacy of reward and punishment for these two types of people. For the faithful, rewards are evident and tangible in this world. The author of Ben Sira explains:

> Good things and bad, life and death,
> poverty and wealth, come from the Lord.
> The Lord's gift remains with the devout,
> and his favor brings lasting success. . . .
> The blessing of the Lord is the reward of the pious,
> and quickly God causes his blessing to flourish. (Sirach
>   11:14–17, 22)

The reward might be in the form of offspring, financial gain or property, wisdom, or status, but all rewards are in the here and now. There is no sense that the faithful might be denied their due, nor that the evil might go unpunished with immediate consequences for their unfaithfulness. Instead, the wisdom tradition affirms that the good things that happen in this world are a sign of favor and proof of righteousness, while curses and hurt are a sign of damnation.

Since most of these texts focus on immediate reward and punishment, an afterlife or place of eternal torment or bliss is never mentioned. The wisdom writers mention heaven only as the place where God and the angels dwell, and they do not talk about a blissful life to come for the faithful, except perhaps in the memories of the living (as in Wisd. of Sol. 8:13). They may mention Sheol, (as in Job 7:9, Prov. 1:12, and others) but only as a sort of holding cell for the dead, without regard to one's actions in life.

> *Sheol* is the common term in the Old Testament for the underworld. The people who wrote the Bible believed the earth was flat and that it was squeezed between a world above (heaven) and a world below (Sheol, see Isa. 7:11). In the Bible, Sheol is described as the place people go when they die, whether righteous or wicked (see Ezek. 32 and Ps. 88).

Consider other examples from the wisdom tradition, such as this from the book of Ecclesiastes:

> For the fate of humans and the fate of animals is the same; as one dies, so dies the other. They all have the same breath, and humans have no advantage over the animals; for all is vanity. All go to one place; all are from the dust, and all turn to dust again. (3:19–20)

And similarly from the book of Job:

> Remember that my life is a breath;
>   my eye will never again see good.
> The eye that beholds me will see me no more;
>   while your eyes are upon me, I shall be gone.
> . . . For now I shall lie in the earth;
>   you will seek me, but I shall not be. (7:7–8, 21)

In wisdom literature, then, what one experiences in this life is all one has. What one gains, one gains here, and death marks the end of striving and self. In the end, all are dust, and all turn to dust again.

Apocalyptic texts depend on the ideals of justice, order, and good and evil that we see in these wisdom texts. Once Israel fell under the imperial domination of the Assyrians, Neo-Babylonians, Persians, Greeks, and Romans, the simple answers of the wisdom texts could no longer respond to the pressures imposed by other nations. As part of the efforts to truly conquer the people they subjugated, these empires enacted policies that had an impact on the law of Judaism, and consequently on a person's ability to keep it. By the time of Greek rule, for example, laws were enacted banning circumcision and compelling the Jewish people to eat unclean foods. People who refused were killed in horrific ways (e.g., 2 Macc. 7). In the later Roman occupation, many Jews and Christians were pressured to give up monotheistic practice for the Roman tradition of emperor worship. In Asia Minor during the reign of Domitian (81–96 CE), for example, the imperial cult was at least promoted and may have even been compulsory, with Domitian himself demanding to be called "Lord and God." Such a violation of monotheistic principles may have been part of the motivation for the writing of the Revelation in the New Testament.

A system whereby those that kept the law of Moses and meditated on wisdom were blessed with righteousness and gain in this lifetime, and whereby the good could trust that they would be rewarded and the evil would be punished, could no longer address the realities of the world of subjugation and oppression and left people struggling for understanding. People were asking, "Does Greek rule mean that the Greeks are favored by God? But how could they be favored when they so clearly flout the Law?" And what of the Jewish people who tried to keep Torah, only to be tortured or killed for their faithfulness? Did they deserve to die? The wisdom worldview simply could not answer these questions in meaningful ways for oppressed people, and gradually a new view of the world came into existence to address some of these key questions.

CHARACTERISTICS OF APOCALYPTIC LITERATURE

The earliest forms of apocalyptic literature appear ca. 200 BCE when the former kingdoms of Israel and Judah were under Greek rule. Over several hundred years, the features of apocalyptic literature grew and developed into what we see in Jewish and Christian texts today. However, all apocalyptic texts do not share all characteristics of apocalyptic literature; instead, they share a common ideology. Jewish and Christian apocalyptic texts are different because the beliefs and practices of the religions differ.

An *ideology* is a worldview or way of thinking. Everyone views the world differently, of course, but sometimes people with similar experiences share a similar way of thinking about those experiences. In the case of apocalyptic communities, shared suffering results in an ideology which looks forward to the end of suffering.

I will try to make clear these theological differences as we go. Finally, scholars differentiate between the following:

- apocalyptic literature
- apocalyptic worldview
- apocalypticism

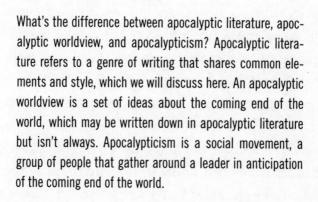

What's the difference between apocalyptic literature, apocalyptic worldview, and apocalypticism? Apocalyptic literature refers to a genre of writing that shares common elements and style, which we will discuss here. An apocalyptic worldview is a set of ideas about the coming end of the world, which may be written down in apocalyptic literature but isn't always. Apocalypticism is a social movement, a group of people that gather around a leader in anticipation of the coming end of the world.

These categories are used because texts cannot and do not contain all aspects of a group's ideology. In fact, not all apocalyptic communities (in the sense of having a dire view of a fast-approaching end) produce apocalyptic works, so I will emphasize the literature's genre (or, conventional style of writing in apocalyptic literature) because it is the writings and the ideas they contain that continue to influence historical and modern apocalyptic movements.

GENRE

The most widespread feature of apocalyptic literature is this: apocalyptic texts develop in situations of oppression and/or uncertainty. The crisis may be political or theological, and it may be real or perceived, but behind most apocalyptic literature is a group of people asking why. As previously discussed, after the destruction of the first temple, Jewish life was difficult. Not only did the Babylonians destroy the sacred space in Jerusalem, where God was said to dwell; they also ended the Davidic monarchy, which was supposed to have stood forever (see 2 Sam. 7) and sent the people into exile far from the land of Judah. Even after the temple was rebuilt and the people returned under the Persian emperor Cyrus, no leader from the line of David was allowed to rule. Instead, foreign emperors appointed client or puppet kings to oversee subjugated lands. These rulers were often brutal in their treatment of the local population, as exemplified by the Greek Seleucid princes in the second century BCE.

The Seleucids were a series of Greek rulers that controlled Palestine from 223–164 BCE. They got their name from the first of these leaders, Seleucus I, who had been a general of the Greek conqueror Alexander the Great.

Among the most vicious of the Seleucids was Antiochus IV, who ruled from 175–164 BCE. According to the stories in the apocryphal books of the Maccabees, Antiochus expected more than just political obedience and taxes from the people; he demanded to be called Epiphanes ("God manifest") and forbade the Jewish people from circumcision, kosher, and worship in the temple (2 Macc. 6) in order to make the people behave like Greeks. This is a process called Hellenization, and usually refers to making language, philosophy, art, and/or religion more Greek.

The Apocrypha is a collection of ancient texts that are revered and used in worship by Christians in the Roman Catholic and Orthodox traditions. Included in this collection are writings such as Tobit, Judith, 1 and 2 Maccabees, Wisdom of Solomon, Ecclesiasticus, and Baruch, along with additions to other books of the Canon such as Daniel and Esther. These books aren't part of the Protestant Canon, but do help all Christians understand the social and historical situation right before the life of Jesus.

When he heard of potential rebellion, he "ordered his soldiers to cut down without mercy those [Judeans] whom they saw and to slay those who took refuge in their houses" (2 Macc. 5:12). At one point Antiochus's army even marched into the temple and sacrificed to Zeus on the altar there. The Jewish rebellion that followed this desecration of the temple is remembered in the eight-night celebration of Hanukkah, with one candle lit for each night the people needed in order to make the temple a sacred space again.

Apocalyptic sections of Daniel (specifically 7–12) address this time of persecution by looking forward to a time when suffering will be resolved. Here is one vision:

> I saw one like a human being coming with the clouds of heaven. And he came to the Ancient One and was presented before him. To him was given dominion and glory and kingship, that all peoples, nations, and languages should serve him. (Dan. 7:13–14)

You can see that both the religious and political uncertainty of the time is addressed by imagining a new (soon-to-come) king, approved by God (the "Ancient One") and appointed to rule over all people, including foreign oppressors. It is no wonder that, during this period and other times of persecution or uncertainty, it became necessary to rethink the past worldview of the wisdom literature and the absolutism of a Davidic monarchy, which didn't last forever as planned. Apocalypticism became a way to imagine hope in such bleak times, to provide assurance that current conditions were soon to end.

Many scholars point out that not all apocalyptic literature can be traced to a particular moment of political crisis. Instead, as previously mentioned, uncertainties about God, life, and death can result in apocalyptic writing. One common concern, it seems, is the fate of the dead. The Pentateuch makes no mention of a life after death; the prophets and writings (except the apocalyptic sections of Daniel) share little more. In some books that follow Deuteronomy the authors mention Sheol, but only as an abode of all the dead. Reward for the righteous or a punishment for the wicked in Sheol is not discussed. As we have seen, wisdom literature tended to emphasize present rewards for the righteous and present punishment for the unjust.

By the Hellenistic period, authors address the injustice of an immediate reward and punishment system. Obviously, a Hellenistic writer would not be able to ignore his own situation where the innocent were slaughtered and the heretics ruled. Key issues needing to be addressed would include the following:

💣 How to still trust in an orderly world

💣 How to maintain the hope that the murdered were not gone forever without reward for their faithfulness

The answer was that rewards and punishments happened in the vast space and time of eternity—not in the relative space and time of earthly nation-states. Consider the following text from Daniel:

> At that time [of anguish] your people shall be delivered, everyone who is found written in the book. Many of those who sleep in the dust of the earth shall awake, some to everlasting life, and some to shame and everlasting contempt. Those who are wise shall shine like the brightness of the sky, and those who lead many to righteousness, like the stars for ever and ever. (12:1–3)

Here, we see a strong connection between righteousness and reward, as did our wisdom tradition, but the time of the deliverance for the just is pushed forward, to the end of the time of anguish. Those who are already dead (the ones that sleep) will rise to life and be judged according to their wisdom and righteousness, leading to everlasting reward or punishment.

Sleep is a common Hellenistic euphemism for death. There is discussion among biblical scholars about where those rewarded in Daniel end up. This passage may imply that they become stars—an astral afterlife. It's not surprising that the author of Daniel 12 would think about ascent to the stars as a potential afterlife. Greek authors such as Cicero, ca. 200 BCE, described eternity by stating, "You see, humans are brought into existence in order to inhabit the earth, which is at the center of this holy place, this paradise. They have been given souls made out of the undying fire which make up stars and constellations, consisting of spherical bodies animated by the divine mind, each moving with marvelous speed, each in its own orbit and cycle . . . Such is the life that leads to heaven, and to the company of those who, having finished their lives in the world, are now freed from their bodies and dwell in that region you gaze upon, the Milky Way."

The distressed had hope that all would be set right and the rewards reaped from endurance would be everlasting.

ANTICIPATING THE MESSIAH

One particular concern of the apocalyptic audience crossed over the boundaries of both political and theological distress, namely the fate of the temple and Davidic line of kings. Earlier we saw that the first temple was destroyed by the Babylonians and rebuilt under Persian rule, and that this second temple was desecrated under the Hellenistic ruler Antiochus IV. Later, this second temple would also be destroyed by the Romans, never to be built again. Since the time of the Babylonian destruction of that first temple, no member of the Davidic line had ruled over Jerusalem, the temple's holy city, in spite of the fact that a Davidic king had been promised to dwell in Zion forever (see 2 Sam. 7:13). In apocalyptic texts this covenant promise for an eternal Davidic king shifts into the future, when one anointed like David would overthrow the oppressor and rule forever.

The word for *anointed one* in Hebrew is *meshiakh*, from which comes the term *Messiah* or *Christ* in Greek.

Many Jews anticipated the coming of this messiah to end the political persecution and religious uncertainty that plagued them; early Christians, who believed Jesus to be this messiah, still waited for his return, as he had not in his lifetime overthrown the powers of this world.

Messianic anticipation is clearly evident in the Jewish texts known as the Dead Sea Scrolls:

The Dead Sea Scrolls are a large collection of writings discovered in 1947 near the Dead Sea in southern Israel. These scrolls were likely written between 250 BCE–70 CE by a community of Jewish people known as Essenes, who had escaped into the desert area around the Dead Sea to avoid persecution by the Romans. To date, we have unearthed nearly two hundred scrolls from this area. Some scrolls are copies of biblical texts, such as Isaiah or Daniel. Some are interpretations of the Bible, known as *pesharim*, and some are rules for the community members.

[The hea]vens and the earth will obey His Messiah [. . . and all th]at is in them. He will not turn aside from the commandments of the holy ones. Take strength in His service (you) who seek the Lord. Will you not find the Lord in this, all you who wait patiently in your hearts? For the Lord will visit the pious ones, and the righteous ones He will call by name. Over the meek His Spirit will hover, and the faithful He will restore by His power. He will glorify the pious ones on the throne of the eternal kingdom. He will release the captives, make the blind see, raise up the downtrodden. For[ev]er I shall cling to him . . . and [I shall trust] in His loving kindness, and [His] goodness of holiness and will not delay. And as for the wonders that are not the work of the Lord, when He [. . .] then he will heal the slain, resurrect the dead, and announce glad tidings to the poor. He will lead the [hol]y ones; he will shepherd [th]em; he will do and all of it. (4Q521)

Notice that here, as elsewhere in apocalyptic literature, the messiah comes to play a dual role: (1) he establishes a never-ending kingdom, and (2) he participates in the final judgment, resurrection of the dead, and recreation of a more just world. In this one figure then, many apocalyptic writers were able to address both the political and theological concerns of their communities with hope.

This desire to sustain hope in distressing circumstances, and the pushing forward of reward and punishment, lead us to a second critical feature of apocalyptic literature.

Today we often see movies portraying this event as some world-ending cosmic explosion or some massive alien invasion that destroys us all. In general, ancient apocalyptic writers viewed the *eschaton* (end) as a time of renewal. Evil would be overthrown, certainly, but that did not mean there would no longer be a heaven or an earth. Two examples, nearly two hundred years apart, illustrate this.

> THE APOCALYPTIC WORLDVIEW IMAGINES A COMING END TO EVIL AND OPPRESSION, USUALLY IN THE IMMEDIATE FUTURE.

In the book of Enoch, a Jewish pseudepigraphal text likely written in the Hellenistic period, the author has a vision of the ages that have passed, and then the one that is soon to come. He writes:

> [God] will execute vengeance among the angels.
> And the first heaven shall depart and pass away,
> And a new heaven shall appear,
> And all the powers of the heaven shall give sevenfold light.
> . . . And all shall be in goodness and righteousness,
> And sin shall no more be mentioned forever. (1 Enoch 94:17)

In this first text, we see that the heavenly realm shall be purged of any unrighteous angels in what the author earlier calls "the great eternal judgment." However, the heavens do not cease to exist but are restored to an even greater glory.

A few hundred years later, during the Roman occupation, the book of Revelation expresses the eschaton this way:

> Then I saw a new heaven and a new earth; for the first heaven and the first earth had passed away, and the sea was no more. . . . And I heard a loud voice from the throne say-ing . . . "God himself will be with them; he will wipe every tear from their eyes. Death will be no more." (21:1, 3–4)

Here, both heaven and earth are re-created like a new genesis when evil (imagined as the Sea [think Gen. 1] and Death) is overthrown and destroyed. Again, the understanding is not that the world will be destroyed in a fiery ball, never to return. Aliens aren't mentioned as leveling all of civilization. Instead, the old world—both heaven and earth—must "pass away" to make way for a new, better world where oppression, pain, and death no longer exist.

Keep in mind that for the ancient apocalyptic writers and their audiences the world was coming to an end very soon. In the face of oppression such as that experienced by Jews and Christians of the Greco-Roman world, there was little to no hope that would result from a prediction of the end that would not come for thousands of years. Instead, the hope and comfort of apocalypticism came from an assurance of imminent deliverance from suffering. While it was not uncommon to place the setting of an apocalypse in the distant past, the warnings and exhortations were for the present age.

Consider, for example, Paul's apocalypse in 1 Thessalonians. Paul was a Christian of the Roman Empire, who related the apocalypse to his own understanding of Jesus as the messiah who was resurrected and would return from heaven to deliver believers and bring about the end of this evil age. Paul wrote to fellow Christians in Thessalonika:

> So that you may not grieve as others do who have no hope. . . . we declare to you by the word of the Lord, that we who are alive, who are left until the coming of the Lord, will by no means precede those who have died. For the Lord himself, with a cry of command, with the archangel's call and with the sound of God's trumpet, will descend from heaven, and the dead in Christ will rise first. Then we who are alive, who are left, will be caught up in the clouds together with them. (1 Thess. 4:13, 15–17)

Paul does not think the *parousia* will be thousands of years in the making as he himself will be alive when it occurs (4:15, 17).

Parousia means "arrival" in Greek, and for early Christians it most often referred to the anticipated return of Jesus to judge humankind.

It is Paul's firm conviction here that the apocalyptic judgment is coming so soon that many of his generation (himself included) will see it in their lifetimes. It is by the assurance of this imminent end that the early Christians found hope in the midst of grief.

As part of eschatological expectation, many apocalyptic visionaries imagined the coming end of evil to be signaled by events or persons in the present reality. We saw in the excerpt from 1 Thessalonians that, for Paul, one of these signals is the bodily resurrection of the dead (although not all people believed in bodily resurrection at this time). It was also common for an apocalyptic visionary to see present political oppression as a sign of the end, along with natural calamities (like earthquakes and famines), wars, and cosmic portents (such as astrological formations). And, as we have already mentioned, the Jewish idea of a messianic figure was likely to be associated with the coming of the new age.

The texts above have already given us a glimpse of a third common feature of apocalypticism in the ancient world: apocalyptic authors see the world in terms of cosmic dualism. Cosmic dualism is the belief that the whole universe, including the heavens and the earth, is divided between forces which work for good and those which plot evil. The cosmic orientation of apocalyptic writings is evident in the easy way in which the person having the vision moves between realms, taking journeys through the heavens and across time. Apocalypses often lay out the whole course of history in front of that individual, culminating in a vision of the near future when good will finally and completely triumph over evil. Evil marks this current age, but the age to come will be dominated by goodness and righteousness. Humans are participants in this dualism, of course, but the scope of the apocalyptic vision is always larger than just the earth or its human inhabitants. Instead, it is a vision of angels and monsters, realms of torment and realms of bliss. Many apocalyptic movies portray the end of the world with battles between angels and demons. As we saw in the earlier example from Revelation, both earth and the heavens participate in the re-creation of the world. The whole cosmos takes part in accomplishing this task.

How large is the world as imagined by the apocalyptic author, and how evenly divided? Consider the Apocalypse of Abraham, a Jewish text, which was likely written about the same time as Revelation (late first century CE). In it, God calls out to the patriarch Abraham to witness visions of the coming judgment.

> And [God] said to me [Abraham], "Look now beneath your feet at the firmament and understand the creation that was depicted of old on this expanse, and the creatures which are in it and the age prepared after it. And I looked beneath the firmament at my feet and I saw the likeness of heaven and the things that were therein. And I saw there the earth and its fruit, and its moving things . . . and its host of men and the impiety of their souls and their justification, and their pursuit of their works and the abyss and its torments, and its lower depths and the perdition in it. And I saw there the sea and its islands . . . and Leviathan and his realm and his bed and his lairs, and the world which lay upon him . . . And I saw there the garden of Eden and its fruits . . . and I saw there a great crowd of men and women and children, half of them on the right side of the portrayal, and half of

them on the left side of the portrayal. . . . "These who are on the left side are a multitude of tribes who existed previously and after you some who have been prepared for judgment and order, others for revenge and perdition at the end of the age. Those on the right side of the picture are the people set apart for me of the people with Azazel; these are the ones I have prepared to be born of you and to be called my people." (ApocAb. 21–22)

The scope of this vision is grand and ranges from the earth, the heavens, the underworld, the sea, the mythical beasts, and finally to the people. In the apocalypse humans are divided into two camps. Those on the left are destined for judgment, and those on the right to be the people of God.

These two camps are locked in conflict with each other. The assurance of the apocalypse is that good will ultimately (but not yet) prevail. When good is triumphant, all will be judged; those on the side of good will be raised to eternal life, and those on the side of evil will suffer eternal torment. However, before such judgment can sort the camps for eternity, the forces of unrighteousness appear to be winning. In the above example from the Apocalypse of Abraham, those on the left attack those on the right, capturing and slaughtering the people and destroying the temple (ApocAb. 27). In the midst of this vision, Abraham cries out, "Why?" and "How long?"—two common utterances in apocalyptic visions (see Dan, 12:6; Rev. 6:10). To each cry, God assures Abraham that "the time of justice will come upon them" and "my judgment will come upon the heathen" (ApocAb. 27:11; 29:14).

THE PURPOSE OF SYMBOLISM

During this period oppressed people could not openly write to describe the judgment and overthrow of a ruler or ruling empire. Needless to say, kings and emperors would likely be very displeased. An apocalyptic author would protect himself and his community by hiding criticism in the form of fantastical visions that concealed hidden meaning for the intended audience.

Apocalyptic literature is characterized by imagery, metaphor, and symbolic language revealed or explained to the visionary by an otherworldly mediator such as an angel.

Symbolic language serves many purposes. As already mentioned, it keeps the outsiders, particularly the oppressors, from gathering the true meaning of the vision. At the same time meaningful symbols, when understood in context, provide a hopeful message that presents a future free from suffering and persecution for community insiders. The Greek word *apocalypsis* means "revealed," and apocalyptic discourse is revelatory in the sense of both revealing a vision to the writer and a plan for redemption to the hearer. Symbolic language allows for multiple meanings in a way that straight prose does not; the author can evoke, with one image, a host of ideas and feelings.

NUMBERS IN JEWISH AND CHRISTIAN APOCALYPSES

The symbolic language in apocalyptic literature comes in many forms. Numbers in the Bible are significant, so it is no surprise that authors used numbers to evoke ideas and feelings in the intended audience. The number seven, for example, is associated in the Old Testament (the Jewish Tanakh) with the completion of the creation in Genesis 2 and the Sabbath, the day of rest from all labor. Because of its association with Sabbath rest and the created order, the authors of Leviticus instituted the resting of land, the release of slaves, and the Jubilee year (when all debts were forgiven) to years in multiples of seven. It is no surprise, then, that seven features prominently in many apocalypses as a reminder of God's power over creation and the rest and restoration that is to come. Sevens appear in the grouping of angels, bowls, and more in apocalyptic texts; the number even occurs in conjunction with scary or dangerous beasts, as in the seven horns of the beast in Daniel. The number must have resonated as a reminder of restoration with the original audience.

Other numbers are also important to the symbolic world of the apocalypticist. Twelve is common; Jews and Christians both found it particularly important because of its association with the twelve tribes that settled the land of Canaan. For Christians, twelve was also significant because of the twelve disciples of Jesus. The association with tribes and disciples indicates a different sort of kingdom, under the reign of God/Christ rather than occupying power. Numbers such as seven and twelve would be powerful comforts and reminders to an audience in distress of God's past protection and presence through time.

ANIMALS AND MYTHICAL BEASTS

Animals and mythical creatures are also standard features in apocalyptic literature. The most frightening of these creatures most often represent kingdoms or rulers opposed to the people for whom the apocalypse was written. Consider this example from Daniel 7. When Daniel does not understand the beasts, the attendant explains:

> As for these four great beasts, four kings shall arise out of the earth. . . . As for the fourth beast, there shall be a fourth kingdom on earth that shall be different from all the other kingdoms; it shall devour the whole earth, and trample it down, and break it to pieces. (Daniel 7:17, 23)

Here the mediating angel interprets Daniel's vision of the beasts to clarify that these refer to kingdoms that were and are to come. The most terrible of the terrible beasts is always the current political power, and this beast is usually described in most detail. As apocalyptic literature evolved through time, some of these terrible beasts were repurposed for a new audience, to refer to a new kingdom. For example, the beasts in Daniel (to refer to Greece) are reused in Revelation to reference Rome. It was also not unusual for apocalypticists to draw on the mythology of the larger context, employing the mythical beasts of Persian, Greek, or Roman culture in their desire to emphasize the truly large-scale nature of the end.

ANGELS

Supernatural beings, especially angels, also play a significant role in the symbolic world of apocalypses. As we have noted, apocalypses are cosmic, meaning they reach beyond the confines of the earth to envision a universe struggling with injustice. It is no surprise, then, that heavenly beings would participate.

Since so much of apocalyptic discourse is symbols and images, the angel often explains the meaning behind the symbol to the visionary, or helps the seer cope with what he has witnessed. At other times, the angel might function as a sort of tour guide, especially in apocalypses with cosmic journeys. The angel or divine agent also often gives direction to the seer, particularly on how to preserve the content of the vision. Usually, the seer is requested to write down the vision, and then to seal it up for the proper time, although in the Christian book of Revelation John is specifically requested not to seal up the vision, since the end is so soon (22:10). Scholars debate the reason a mediator is so often employed in apocalyptic texts. However, the angelic mediator is by far the most common feature in apocalyptic texts and clearly plays a critical role in the interpretive acts within it.

ANGELS SERVE MANY ROLES IN APOCALYPTIC TEXTS, BUT BY FAR THE MOST COMMON IS MEDIATOR OR INTERPRETER.

THE IMPORTANCE OF A GOOD AUTHOR

Apocalyptic texts received their authority based on the author. Often the angelic figure interprets visions for a great figure from the biblical tradition such as Ezra, Abraham, Adam, Daniel, Enoch, and Moses.

JEWISH AND CHRISTIAN APOCALYPSES

Even though texts claim to be written by a great character of the past who hears/sees the vision, records it, and seals it up for a later time, these works were written by unnamed authors in the reader's present time.

1 Enoch	Apocalypse of Adam
2 Enoch	Apocalypse of Abraham
3 Enoch	Apocalypse of Elijah
Apocryphon of Ezekiel	Apocalypse of Daniel
4 Ezra	Testament of Job
2 Baruch	Testament of Abraham
3 Baruch	

Clearly these stories were not written by the figure with which they are associated. They are, therefore, written by authors using pseudonyms—names used to protect the author's identity from the foreign king or empire. The use of a pseudonym is a defining characteristic of apocalypses.

As is true with the symbolic language, pseudonymity functions in several ways, but two are critical to the nature of apocalyptic literature:

1. Pseudonymity protects the actual author of the text.

   Even if no outsider ever read the apocalypse, the real author would certainly be aware that the ideas contained in it would be unpopular or outright seditious to the imperial powers. As such, it made good sense to protect oneself as much as possible.

2. Pseudonymity invests the apocalypse with authority.

   Just ascribing the apocalypse to the great heroes of the biblical tradition in itself gives the apocalypse a certain weight; this power is magnified by projecting the vision into the past and suggesting that the events described were foreseen and have now come to pass. Modern readers often struggle with the concept of pseudonymity, in part because they equate it with plagiarism or lying. However, there is good evidence that pseudonymity was a writing style in antiquity; while it was sometimes seen as disingenuous, this was not always the case.

PUTTING IT ALL TOGETHER

In this section you saw the common characteristics of apocalyptic literature.

- 💣 It is the writing of distressed people.
- 💣 It includes symbolic language, cosmic visions, dualism, and pseudonymity.

💣 It offers comfort to the intended audience and challenges the permanence and power of current political systems.

💣 It speaks to the theological concerns of those who recognize that perhaps justice will not be quick to come in this lifetime.

💣 It grows out of the Jewish wisdom tradition, among others.

KEY APOCALYPTIC TEXTS AND THEIR CONTRIBUTIONS

Below, we will discuss several key texts from both Jewish and Christians sources and offer at least one feature of the text that became important to the genre, or impacted later failed apocalyptic predictions. This is a brief chronological sketch in the service of understanding which ideas and images retained authority for later Jews and Christians, rather than an exhaustive discussion of provenance, authorship, or manuscript traditions. From the Jewish tradition, I have chosen to include excerpts from the books of Enoch, Daniel 7–12, The Community Rule and The War Scroll from Qumran, 4 Ezra, and 2 Baruch. From Christianity I have included 1 Thessalonians and 1 Corinthians from the Pauline corpus, Mark 13, and Revelation. This listing is by no means exhaustive, which may give some readers pause, especially those that thought there was only one view of the end of the world! However, we should be able to discern many of the ideas and images that persisted into modern apocalyptic movements by first offering a brief introduction to these selected texts.

JEWISH TEXTS

As we have already discussed, apocalypticism in Jewish tradition really begins in the period of Greek rule over Judea. From this time period, we draw two of our representative apocalypses: 1 Enoch and Daniel. Of these, scholarly consensus is that 1 Enoch, at least at some points, represents an earlier tradition than Daniel.

First Enoch

First Enoch is actually several independent narratives grouped around the biblical figure of Enoch. In Genesis, Enoch was a forbearer to Noah, and "Enoch walked with God; then he was no more, because God took him" (5:24). The idea that God "took" Enoch made him a peculiar person of particular interest to later visionaries and writers. More than a few apocalyptic works suggest Enoch lived on, going on otherworldly journeys and learning the mysteries of the divine. The traditions associated with Enoch were compiled over several centuries, beginning in the pre–Maccabean period, and eventually including 1 Enoch as well as two other collections (2 and 3 Enoch) likely written in the Roman period.

For our purposes, 1 Enoch is perhaps most notable for being the oldest. Chapters 6–16 are likely the earliest apocalyptic text. This section is sometimes called Book of the Watchers, and it retells and expands a short story from Genesis 6:1–8, in which the "sons of God" take "daughters of humans" as their wives and produce children who are called "warriors of renown" (v. 4). This intermingling of the "sons of God" with humans becomes a cause of the flood in 1 Enoch.

The expansion in the Book of the Watchers suggests that these biblical "sons of God" were actually angels who lusted after human women and fell to earth. Like the titan Prometheus in Greek mythology, these angels brought with them symbols of civilization: swords and weapons, knowledge of astrology and medicine, ornamentation such as jewelry, and alchemy. Other angels oppose these fallen ones, whose gifts from heaven torment humanity. Enoch sees all this in a vision from his hiding place and intercedes on behalf of the fallen angels, finally receiving from God a vision of their judgment. At the end of this vision, God expands the judgment to include all of humanity and all of time, concluding "they [the Watchers] will corrupt until the day of the great conclusion, until the great age is consummated, until everything is concluded" (16:1).

We see the characteristics of apocalyptic literature even in this early text. The text is pseudonymous, with a visionary Enoch standing in for the author. The apocalypse is cosmic, with warring heavenly parties and movement between the human and divine realms. It uses the symbols and images of the cultural contributions of the fallen angels to refer to current problems; in this case, it is likely that these contributions are intended to remind the hearer of the massive cultural differences between the people of Judea and the Hellenistic culture around them. Finally, the vision ends with the assurance of judgment for the wicked.

Despite the fact that Enoch was beloved enough to become attached to three separate apocalypses and revered enough to be seen as an instructive and valuable text to be quoted in the book of Jude (14, 15), Enoch was eventually left out of the Canon. The one apocalyptic book that made it into the bible was Daniel, which contains a large apocalyptic section (chapters 7—12). These apocalyptic chapters in Daniel are characterized by visions and prophetic language, and are set in the reign of Belshazzar during the Persian period (500s BCE). However, the apocalyptic sections of Daniel are not about the Persian period; they look instead to the reign of the Greek king Antiochus IV and are clearly tied to his persecution and defilement of the temple. As with many apocalypses, the visions are placed in the distant but familiar past to protect the actual author and lend authenticity to the prophetic discourse.

The chapters in question are a series of separate revelations given to Daniel, as he "lay in bed" (7:1), prayed (9:3), or fasted (10:3). The early visions include many bizarre animals: a lion with eagle's wings, a bear with three tusks, a beast with iron teeth and eleven horns, and a male goat with uneven horns that tramples a ram. When Daniel does not understand the visions, others explain them as relating to kings and kingdoms that will come "many days from now" (Dan. 8:26). The beast with the eleven horns is given the most explanation, as it represents the Greek empire; the eleventh horn on that beast is Antiochus Epiphanies, who "shall speak words against the

Most High, shall wear out the holy ones of the Most High, and shall attempt to change the sacred seasons and the law" (Dan. 7:25). The later sections of the apocalypse include a confession of Daniel on behalf of the Jewish people, a recitation of history leading up to the time of Antiochus, and a final judgment by Michael at the "time of anguish" (12:1). In his confession and again in the vision of the final judgment, Daniel imagines an "abomination that desolates" in the temple, a clear reference to the improper sacrifices which defiled the temple in the time of Antiochus (9:27; 11:31).

Isaiah 26:19, which predates Daniel, refers to "dwellers in the dust" who will "awake and sing for joy," but this appears to be metaphorical language for the people returning from exile. Even if given the most literal interpretation possible, however, it still does not support a dual judgment on both the righteous and the wicked, as in the apocalyptic tradition.

The book of Daniel represents a significant moment in the development of apocalypticism for several reasons. For one, the judgment includes a reference to the bodily resurrection of both the good and evil dead at the time of judgment. "One in human form" (10:18) explains this event to Daniel in this way:

> There shall be a time of anguish, such as has never occurred since nations first came into existence. But at that time your people shall be delivered, everyone who is found written in the book. Many of those who sleep in the dust of the earth

shall awake, some to everlasting life, and some to shame and everlasting contempt. (12:1–2)

The idea of the bodily resurrection of the dead appears often in the apocalyptic literature of both Jews and Christians. Following the book of Daniel's example, 2 Baruch, the apocalyptic sections of Paul's Corinthian correspondence (especially 1 Cor. 15), and Revelation all reference bodily resurrection. By all accounts, many Jews and Christians from the Hellenistic period onward believed in the literal resurrection of the dead where the person would literally get up out of the ground on the day of reckoning. Either the believer's body was never separate from some eternal part of the self, or it was reunited with the soul at the time of judgment. In the Christian tradition, the most explicit discussion of this event may be in 1 Thessalonians 4:16, 17, where "the dead in Christ will rise first. Then we who are alive . . . will be caught up . . . together with them to meet the Lord in the air." Christians also believed the resurrection of Jesus to be a sort of first example of this general resurrection.

Daniel is also significant to the apocalyptic tradition in that it continues to be a source of inspiration long after the Maccabean period when Antiochus defiled the temple. The eschatological communities that produced the Dead Sea Scrolls, for example, wrote no fewer than eleven texts related to the preservation and interpretation of Daniel (Flint 41). The author of the gospel of Mark refers to the "desolating sacrilege" (13:14) of Daniel 9:27 and 11:31, and transfers this image to the destruction of the second temple by Roman forces 230 years later.

Mark also uses the designation "Son of Man," which in Daniel 7:13 (in many Bible versions) refers to the king, as a title for Jesus throughout his gospel; this title is adopted by the gospels of Matthew and Luke as well as the author of Revelation. Revelation also takes Daniel's four beasts and combines them into one super-beast that might remind us today of a mutant monster out of a movie or comic book. The beast, "having ten horns . . . was like a leopard, its feet were like a bear's, and its mouth was like a lion's mouth" (Rev. 13:1–2). This super-beast, with the most ferocious aspects of Daniel's four beasts, represents Rome, who made "war on the saints . . . to conquer them" (Rev. 13:7).

The Dead Sea Scrolls

Following the rebellion against Antiochus IV, the Jewish people enjoyed a brief period of self-rule, known as the Hasmonean period, which lasted about one hundred years. The leaders of the rebellion, the Maccabean and Hasmonean families, assumed control of both political and religious leadership in Jerusalem, including the temple. However, divisions within the families and alliances with Rome led to internal struggles, which divided the small nation and left it open to conquest. In 63 BCE the Romans, under General Pompey, overtook the temple mount and any vestiges of independence were gone. From this point, Judea was a Roman province.

It was Hasmonean control of the temple that first gave rise to our next set of texts: the Dead Sea Scrolls. These scrolls, found in the caves beside the site of Qumran in Israel, are the writings of an apocalyptic sect of Judaism that escaped Jerusalem during the Hasmonean period. According to the writings discovered from this community, at some point in the Hasmonean period a "wicked priest" took charge of the temple, instituting religious and political changes (particularly to the calendar) that were intolerable to the followers of a certain "Righteous Teacher." From this point the community lived almost continuously in the Judean desert, meditating on the Torah, practicing asceticism, and preparing for a coming battle between the "sons of light" and the "sons of darkness."

Much of the apocalyptic expectation of this community was focused on restoring the temple and religious practice to their proper states, and regaining political control of Jerusalem from those in league with the Roman oppressors. Thus, the Community Rule (abbreviated by scholars as 1QS) mentions two Messianic figures, one of Israel (a political liberator) and one of Aaron (a priestly liberator):

> They [the righteous] shall depart from none of the counsels of the Law to walk in the stubbornness of their hearts, but shall be ruled by the primitive precepts in which the men of the Community were first instructed until there shall come the Prophet and the Messiahs of Aaron and Israel. (1QS IX, 11)

Another scroll, 4QTestamonia, also alludes to two Messiahs, one royal and one priestly, as well as a prophet like Moses (1QS). If we look at the collection as a whole, however, the role of the Messiahs is small. The actual end of the world is to be accomplished in battle by the "sons of light" and the angel Michael; this final war is imagined in The War Scroll, also known as The War of the Sons of Light Against the Sons of Darkness.

The War Scroll (abbreviated 1QM) is an extensive description of the final conflict. It includes descriptions of the weapons of the warring parties, the titles written on various musical instruments used during the battle (such as the trumpets), the participants, locations, and much more. Additionally, 1QM details the smaller battles within the war (seven total) and the time span of the whole battle (49 years, or 7 x 7). The armies meet on six occasions. Three victories go to the sons of light, and three belong to the sons of darkness: the "Kittim" (probably Rome) and Belial (a demon). In the seventh battle:

> [The] banners of the infantry cause their hearts to melt, then the strength of God will strengthen the he[arts of the Sons of Light.] In the seventh lot: the great hand of God shall overcome [Belial and al]l the angels of his dominion, and all the men of [his forces shall be destroyed forever] (1QM I, 14–15)

The Scroll delineates the new (proper) priesthood as it will be installed in the temple in Jerusalem when the victory is finally won.

The Qumranic literature is not technically apocalyptic in the sense of being a vision revealed by a divine agent to a great figure of the past. However, the Dead Sea Scrolls, of which we have only mentioned a tiny fraction, are important to this conversation for several reasons. First, the community itself became a significant model for other apocalyptic movements and communities. The ascetic living, rigorous adherence to the

Bible, and isolationism all continue to be a part of the way apocalyptic groups deal with perceived injustice and oppression.

Second, the Qumran texts emphasize apocalyptic war, as we saw above. Prior to The War Scroll, our examples of the end of the world did not envision warring parties meeting on an earthly battlefield to duel it out for control of the age to come. Instead, a heavenly being (God, Michael) simply handed out justice at the appointed time, separating the righteous and/ or punishing the sinful. But in the Dead Sea Scrolls we see an orientation toward violence, including human violence, as a necessary means to achieving the end of the world order. This idea will reappear in Revelation and will also be significant for many later apocalyptically-oriented movements.

The Qumranic literature is also significant in that it identifies internal religious battles (such as those over the calendar and priesthood) as another potential root of apocalyptic thought. So not only does religious or political conflict with the larger world produce apocalyptic literature that imagines the end of evil; but we can see for the Qumran community it led to a division between themselves (the "Sons of Light") and both their fellow Jews and the Roman occupying force (the "Sons of Darkness"). This happens again and again in apocalyptic communities whose members appear to be on the same "team," religiously at least, but can in fact be each other's worst enemies.

The people of Qumran should have feared the enemy more; in 68 CE the Roman army completely wiped out the community of believers there, but they were able to hide their vast library of texts in the caves surrounding their compound. Their annihilation was part of the Roman response to the First Jewish Revolt, which also resulted in the destruction of the second temple in Jerusalem. Roman suppression of the first Revolt was swift, brutal, and (in the case of the temple) a sign to many Jewish people that the end must be close at hand. Two Jewish apocalyptic texts deal with the fall of the second temple: 4 Ezra and 2 Baruch. They have some literary connections to one other, as both tie the destruction of the temple to the end of the age.

The consensus of scholars is that 4 Ezra (also known as 2 Esdras) is most likely ten or twenty years older than 2 Baruch. The apocalyptic sections of 4 Ezra (chapters 3—14) probably date to about 100 CE; 2 Baruch dates perhaps as late as 120 CE. Since both show evidence of Christian additions, it is likely that they were written and circulated before the Bar Kochba revolt (*OTP* 1:520).

The Bar Kochba revolt was a Jewish rebellion against the Roman government that took place between 132–135 CE. It is named after the leader of the revolt, Simon, who was called Bar Kochba, or "son of a star."

Each text is set after the fall of the first temple to the Babylonians, so both texts have visions set in the distant past. Both texts use a famous person from an earlier time to give the visions authority, so they are both pseudonymous.

A main concern of both of these texts is theodicy. Theodicy is concerned with a very difficult theological question: "Why do bad things happen to good people if God is just?" In both texts, the person receiving the visions mourns what he perceives as God's injustice toward God's people, especially in regard to the destruction of the temple at the hand of the Roman oppressors (here identified as the Babylonians, who destroyed the first temple, rather than Rome, who destroyed the second).

In 4 Ezra, Ezra asks God:

Are the deeds of those who inhabit Babylon any better? Is that why she has gained dominion over Zion? For when I came here I saw ungodly deeds without number, and my soul has seen many sinners during these thirty years. . . . . Are the deeds of Babylon better than those of Zion? (4 Ezra 3:28–32)

Similarly in 2 Baruch 11:1–7, the prophet laments:

O Babylon: If you had lived in happiness and Zion in its glory it would have been a great sorrow to us that you had been equal to Zion. But now, behold, the grief is infinite and the lamentation is unmeasurable, because, behold, you are happy and Zion has been destroyed. Who will judge over these things? Or to whom shall we complain about that which has befallen us?

Each book compares Babylon (Rome) and Zion (Jerusalem), and each expresses confusion about how the prosperity of Rome could possibly continue if God judged other nations according to the standards set for Judah. It is unsurprising that the authors of these texts were struggling to find meaningful answers to these questions in the aftermath of the destruction of Jerusalem thirty years before.

In both 4 Ezra and 2 Baruch, God's justice is delayed. However, both authors ultimately vindicate God, and do so in part by means of visions of a new (heavenly) temple and city which will be restored and last forever. In 4 Ezra, the angel Uriel tells Ezra, "Do not be afraid, and do not let your heart be terrified; but go in and see the splendor [of the new Zion] and the vastness of the building, as far as it is possible for your eyes to see it" (10:55).

And in 2 Baruch, God speaks to Baruch's first complaint, saying:

> Or do you think that this is the city of which I said: On the palms of my hands I have carved you? It is not this building [the temple] that is in your midst now; it is that which will be revealed, with me, that was already prepared from the moment that I decided to create Paradise. (2 Bar. 4:2-3)

New Jerusalem became a central point for apocalyptic literature after 70 CE as an expression of expectation and hope in light of a dire present theological reality. The image of the New Jerusalem became a rallying call for political apocalyptic movements, since restoring Zion/Jerusalem meant reestablishing the Davidic line in the traditional capitol city and religious center. This is very similar to the book of Revelation that dates to around the same time and focuses on the reestablishment of the Holy City. Later this vision of a new world is a theological touchstone for European settlers on the North American continent who saw themselves establishing a New Jerusalem in the New World.

While 2 Baruch and 4 Ezra's use of rebuilt temple imagery represents a new development in apocalypticism, the two texts also retain many of the features found in earlier Jewish apocalypses. Particularly, in both we continue to see the convention of revelation through a mediator or mediators (the angel Uriel in 4 Ezra 4:1–2; God in 2 Bar. 38–39); an emphasis on resurrection of the dead to dual judgment of the righteous and the unrighteous (4 Ezra 7:102–115; 2 Bar. 30:2–5); a view that the current age is the last and worst (4 Ezra 7:62–74; 2 Bar. 32:6); and a messiah or liberator (4 Ezra 7:26–44; 2 Bar. 53, 54). Though there are other apocalypses written after Baruch and Ezra, these two texts are the latest covered here. These are important because they carry on the earlier features of apocalyptic literature that also appear in the Christian apocalypses that influence apocalyptic movements today.

CHRISTIAN TEXTS

Christianity was born from a Jewish worldview during the Roman occupation of Palestine, so it is no wonder that it also shared many Jewish apocalyptic ideals. Those who wrote Christian apocalyptic materials drew on Jewish sources, especially the book of Daniel, and employed apocalyptic conventions such as symbolic language, visions, scenes of judgment, and messianic expectations. One significant difference, obviously, was that Christians believed Jesus of Nazareth to be the promised messiah who would bring about end of the world, while Jews did not. The fact that Jesus didn't fit the expected model of a messiah that liberated the people politically in his lifetime differed from the model of the political liberator in the older Jewish texts. Instead, Christian apocalypses focused on the tradition of a second coming, but this was not the only difference between Jewish apocalypticism and that of early Christians.

In spite of the organization of the New Testament as we now have it, the gospels are not our earliest surviving Christian literature. The writings of Paul are. Paul was a Jewish citizen of the Roman Empire who came to believe Jesus was the messiah in the middle of the first century CE. Paul sent several letters to churches he founded throughout Asia Minor and Greece, and the early church preserved these letters. First Thessalonians and 1 Corinthians are letters of Paul that contain apocalyptic passages; most scholars date 1 Thessalonians to approximately 50 CE, and 1 Corinthians was written approximately five years later. That means that these letters, and their accompanying ideas concerning the end of the world, predate the gospels and the book of Revelation by decades.

Paul's letter to the Thessalonians is a pastoral letter, addressing the concerns of the local congregation who were worried about those in their community who died before the return of Christ. First Thessalonians is not a developed apocalypse such as the Jewish materials we saw. Instead, Paul shares his apocalyptic worldview in response to the concerns of his church. He writes:

> But we do not want you to be uniformed, brothers and sisters, about those who have died, so that you may not grieve as others do who have no hope. For since we believe that Jesus died and rose again, even so, through Jesus, God will bring with him those who have died. For this we declare to you by the word of the Lord, that we who are alive, who are left until the coming of the Lord, will by no means precede those who have died. For the Lord himself, with a cry of command, with the archangel's call and with the sound of God's trumpet, will descend from heaven, and the dead in Christ will rise first. (1 Thess. 4:13–16)

In this first part of Paul's discussion of the end of the age, we see that the apostle draws on the resurrection of the dead tradition we saw in Jewish texts, though his interpretation lacks the double judgment we saw in Daniel. We can't step back in time and know why Paul only discussed the fate of the believers. It could be that judgment against evil was not part of his worldview, or it may simply be in keeping with the pastoral nature of the letter addressed to a community concerned with the fate of their fellow believers. After all, Paul was addressing that concern, so that they might "encourage one another with these words" (1 Thess. 4:18). Still, the description is quite short and to the point; Paul simply asserts that the dead in Christ will rise and join the living to "meet the Lord in the air" (v. 17).

Paul provides only slightly more discussion of the resurrection of the dead in 1 Corinthians. Again, it appears he is responding to a concern of the community, as he opens the conversation with a question he has heard "someone" ask:

"How are the dead raised? With what kind of body do they come?" Fool! [Paul replies]. . . . So it is with the resurrection of the dead. What is sown is perishable, what is raised is imperishable. It is sown in dishonor, it is raised in glory. . . . It is sown a physical body, it is raised spiritual body. If there is a physical body, there is also a spiritual body. (1 Cor. 15:35–36, 42–44)

Because Paul was a Roman addressing a community in the Greek world, his description of the resurrection relies on allegory, a Greek philosophical way of communication in which one thing is compared to another. Here, just as the plant that grows from the ground does not look like the seed that was planted, so the resurrected body does not look like the body in death. However, Paul continues to claim that it is a body, even though it is a "spiritual body" that will meet the end of days. He concludes, "We will not all die, but we will all be changed in a moment, in the twinkling of an eye, at the last trumpet . . . and the dead will be raised imperishable" (1 Cor. 15:51–52).

The angel's trumpet to signal the resurrection and the end of the world appears in both of Paul's letters. However, in the brief discussion in 1 Corinthians, Paul does not make much of Jesus' role, whereas that is a central preoccupation of his earlier letter. Indeed, in 1 Thessalonians Paul affords the role of raiser of the dead to "the Lord," by which he means the resurrected Jesus. He describes Jesus descending from heaven, to take first the dead and then the living (including, Paul believes, himself) into the clouds. We ought to note that this marks a significant departure from Jewish apocalyptic texts, where this role was often played by an archangel, such as Michael (see Dan. 12, for example). It marks a clear distinction between Jewish and Christian apocalyptic visions like Paul's, too, because it relies on the idea of a returning Jesus as a sign of the end of the age, rather than the first appearance of a messiah as the indicator.

Paul's discussion of the day of the Lord in 1 Thessalonians continues by addressing another apparent concern of the community: When will this world end? To this Paul responds:

> Now concerning the times and the seasons, brother and sisters, you do not need to have anything written to you. For you yourselves know very well that the day of the Lord will come like a thief in the night. When they say, "There is peace and security," then sudden destruction will come upon them, as labor pains come upon a pregnant woman, and there will be no escape! (1 Thess. 5:1-3)

Paul emphasizes the suddenness and unpredictability of the end, using imagery of thieves and labor pains. While Paul has already indicated that he believes the resurrection of the dead will happen in his lifetime, he does not make a claim to know when the "day of the Lord" will be, and apparently trusts that the community at Thessalonika know the same. We see similar language in 1 Corinthians, where the day of resurrection will come "in a moment, in the twinkling of an eye" (15:52).

It is interesting to compare these early Pauline texts to 2 Thessalonians, which paints a quite different picture of the end and was written much later than 1 Thessalonians. In this letter we read a lengthy discussion of the signs leading to the eschaton. Whereas in 1 Thessalonians the end will be completely unexpected and occur quite soon, the author of 2 Thessalo-nians cautions the reader to watch for a long procession of events (2:1–12) which will all precede the end, including a rebellion, the unbinding and revelation of a "lawless one" (v. 3), the exaltation of this lawless one in the temple, a cosmic con-frontation with Jesus, and a delusion sent from God to afflict those who take pleasure in unrighteousness.

In one of the strangest moments in Christian apocalyptic lit-erature, the confrontation between Jesus and the lawless one ends when Jesus destroys him "with the breath of his mouth, annihilating him" (2 Thess. 2:8). Today we might think that is some seriously bad breath.

The author of 2 Thessalonians encourages his reader to not be alarmed or distressed "that the day of the Lord is already here" (2:2), an allusion to the fast approach of the eschaton dis-cussed in letters like 1 Thessalonians and 1 Corinthians.

Clearly, the time between 1 and 2 Thessalonians was marked by Roman persecution of Christians who were waiting for jus-tice to be served when the world ended. Paul's conviction that the end would come in his lifetime, quickly, and with a reward for the faithful didn't happen; Paul died, the Empire seemed to get stronger, and many more Christians were martyred. Then, the fall of the temple in Jerusalem in 70 CE also affected early Christians, many of whom considered themselves to be Jews. The gospel of Mark, likely written around the same time as the destruction of the second temple, sees this event as a clear sign that the world is ending.

Mark is, first and foremost, an account of the "good news of Jesus Christ" (Mark 1:1). Overall, the book is not a full-fledged apocalypse but is instead a narrative of the ministry and execution of Jesus of Nazareth and what those events meant to an early Christian community. The book includes miracle stories, parables, a passion narrative (the suffering of Jesus prior to his execution), and an apocalypse (Mark 13).

This apocalyptic section begins with Jesus' words concerning the fate of the temple: "Not one stone will be left here upon another; all will be thrown down" (13:2). When the disciples hear it, they ask, "When will this be, and what will be the sign that all these things are about to be accomplished?" (v. 4) Here is the interpretation in the book of Mark:

> As for yourselves, beware. . . . Brother will betray brother to death, and a father his child, and children will rise against parents and have them put to death; and you will be hated by all because of my name. But the one who endures to the end will be saved. But when you see the desolating sacrilege set up where it ought not to be (let the reader understand), then those in Judea must flee to the mountains. . . . Woe to those who are pregnant and to those who are nursing infants in those days! Pray that it may not be in winter. For in those days there will be suffering, such as has not been from the beginning of the creation that God created until now, no, and never will be. . . . And if anyone says to you at that time, "Look! Here is the Messiah!" or "Look! There he is!"—do not believe it. False messiahs and false prophets will appear

and produce signs and omens, to lead astray, if possible, the elect. But be alert; I have already told you everything. But in those days, after that suffering, the sun will be darkened, and the moon will not give its light, and the stars will be falling from heaven, and the powers in the heavens will be shaken. Then they will see "the Son of Man coming in clouds" with great power and glory. Then he will send out the angels, and gather his elect from the four winds, from the ends of the earth to the ends of heaven. (Mark 13:9, 12–14, 17–19, 21–27)

This mini-apocalypse in Mark 13 bears many apocalyptic features: cosmological signs, indicators of desperate political and personal circumstances, and the coming of a messianic figure to deliver the righteous. It also draws on earlier apocalyptic tradition, particularly Daniel, quoting the "desolating sacrilege" and "Son of Man" language. In Mark, however, these features refer to the destruction of the second temple by Rome rather than the desecration under Antiochus IV.

Mark presents us with something new—false messiahs and prophets in the community, who are seeking to lead the elect astray. This concept of a false messiah appears in many Christian apocalyptic texts, and generally its dual role is to oppose the truth and signal the end. We saw such a figure in 2 Thessalonians, for example ("the lawless one"). We will see it in Revelation, and in 1 and 2 John the opposing force is actually many "antichrists" (1 John 2:18) who deceive and "do not confess that Jesus Christ has come in the flesh" (2 John 7). With opposition to Christianity it is understandable that the community wondered why the Christian message was being met with antagonism.

Revelation is the final book of the Christian New Testament, and it is the only full-length apocalypse in the Canon. The book is also known as the Apocalypse of John. The book is so rich in symbolism and the visions are so involved that it is hard in an overview to do justice to explaining the visions. However, since so many failed apocalyptic predictions in later years depend on an interpretation of Revelation, we must take time to understand the social situation the book was written during as well as the structure and key images in the book.

Revelation was likely written near the end of the first century CE, but not everyone can agree on an exact date. It is definitely in its final form post-70. Unlike many apocalypses, the visionary author did not employ pseudonymity; instead, he identified himself as "[Jesus Christ's] servant John, who testified to the word of God and to the testimony of Jesus Christ" (Rev. 1:1, 2) from the island of Patmos (1:9). And, from the first vision, the "word" is clear: "Do not be afraid [the Son of Man declares]; I am the first and the last, and the living one. I was dead, and see, I am alive forever and ever; and I have the keys of Death and of Hades" (Rev. 1:17–18).

It is difficult for us today to put ourselves in the world of ancient persecuted Christians, so it may seem confusing to you that the point of the book as stated here is not to terrorize the community but to comfort them with the all-encompassing power of Christ. We can see the theme reinforced in both the structure and the key symbols John uses.

Elisabeth Schussler Fiorenza, a prominent scholar on the book of Revelation, has suggested we view the structure of the book as a sort of "Russian doll in which several other dolls are nestled" (36). At the very beginning (1:1–8) and again at the very end (22:10–21), the author identifies himself like someone would in an ancient letter. Inside this framework, images and ideas in various sections mirror each other. For example, the plagues in Revelation 6–8 mirror those in chapters 15–16. The crises in the seven cities in chapters 1–3 are resolved in the image of the city of God in chapters 21–22, and so on. Schussler Fiorenza points out this structure is not intended to be read in a strictly linear way. Leonard L. Thompson agrees and notes that the unity of repeated images, particularly liturgical images (53–70), gives the book structure. This means that the visions and images presented are meant to reinforce the same ideas from various vantage points; the events contained within it are not necessarily sequential, but instead refer to and rely on each other to provide the most complete vision of the new heaven and new earth John imagines.

MUCH LIKE THE BOOK OF DANIEL, JOHN'S APOCALYPSE IS POPULATED WITH FANTASTIC (AND OCCASIONALLY TERRIBLE) BEASTS AND CREATURES.

John reinforces his message that the believers not fear by relying heavily on the important biblical numbers seven and twelve. Seven, the number that recalls the completion of creation in Genesis 2:2 and the establishment of the Sabbath as the day of rest, appears in Revelation. Seven churches and their seven angels are addressed at the opening of the revelation. A slaughtered Lamb opens seven seals, which release horses and horsemen, as well as revealing martyrs and causing all manner of cosmic calamities. Seven angels blow seven trumpets, releasing additional disasters in the heavens and on earth; seven more angels bring seven plagues. Even though the situations in which the number occurs are horrific in presentation, the inclusion of the number functions as a reminder that the vision and the world are moving toward completion—the end of evil and the beginning of rest. The number twelve appears in the discussion of the sealed servants of God in Revelation 7, where 12 thousand from each of the twelve tribes are represented. Twelve is symbolic of both the land of Israel (from the twelve tribes that settled there after the Exodus) and the origins of the church (in the twelve apostles). Again, in spite of the rather scary context in which the number occurs, the repetitive use of twelve is meant to reinforce John's fundamental themes of redemption and the eventual triumph of the chosen people.

Twelve times 12 thousand equals 144,000, which becomes a significant number to many apocalypse-oriented groups. Among them are the Jehovah's Witnesses, who take the sealing of the 144,000 quite literally, claiming only that number will ultimately be saved.

Much like the book of Daniel, John's apocalypse is populated with fantastic (and occasionally terrible) beasts and creatures. And, like Daniel, John often uses these beasts to stand in for adversaries, kingdoms, and rulers. Among the most prominent and certainly terrible beasts in the apocalypse are the dragon of chapter 12 and the twin beasts of chapter 13. The dragon appears as a part of the cosmic birth of the messiah to the celestial mother, to "devour her child as soon as it was born" (12:4). It is red, with seven heads, ten horns, a tail that could knock the stars from heaven, and the ability to pour water from its mouth. When the child is saved from its jaws, the dragon and its angels make war in heaven and are cast out onto the earth. The fall of Satan and his angels is actually part of the end of the world. The water dragon is a common image in Jewish literature, representing chaos and destructive powers opposed to God in such texts as Job 41 and Psalm 74. Here, John builds on this tradition, later calling the dragon "that ancient serpent, who is the Devil and Satan" (Rev. 20:2). Van Henton also notes that the dragon was a key player in imperial cult myths, and that the usage of dragon imagery here inverts or reverses the expected role of the dragon to become part of John's overall message of imperial overthrow (181–201).

The two beasts of Revelation 13 serve the dragon after his fall. One arises from the sea, the other from the earth. The first, a combination of the worst features of Daniel's four beasts, is worshipped and followed by the whole earth in spite of uttering "blasphemies against God, blaspheming his name and his dwelling" (13:6). In a subsequent chapter, it carries "Babylon the great, mother of whores" (17:5) on its back; the angel mediating the vision says the beast "was, and is not, and is about to ascend from the bottomless pit and go to destruction" (17:8). The second beast acts as an enforcer or deputy for the first. "It exercises all the authority of the first beast on its behalf, and it makes the earth and its inhabitants worship the first beast" (Rev. 13:12). In that role, the second beast sets up images of the first beast (13:14). It also marks all the people with the number 666, without which they are unable to buy or sell anything (Rev. 13:16–18).

These two beasts likely reminded the original audience of Rome and her emperors. In the text itself, the angel interprets the seven heads of the first beast to be "seven mountains on which the [whore of Babylon] is seated; also, they are seven kings" (17:9), referring to the seven hills of Rome. The use of Babylon is significant too because it was common to use Babylon (destroyer of the first temple) as a stand-in for Rome (destroyer of the second). Further, the blasphemies the first beast speaks are often understood to refer to the divine titles used in the Imperial cult, and the images set up by the second as statues of the emperors. The "mark of the beast" may be a numerical representation of Nero Caesar, or may be taken to refer to the inability to buy or sell anything in the empire without using coins stamped with the emperor's face.

It is significant, then, that many of the scenes in the second half of the apocalypse retell some aspect of the power and/ or the destruction of the dragon, his beasts, and the whore of Babylon. As previously mentioned, the structure of John is not exactly linear; it is moving toward an eschatological future by means of reference and replay. So, we see that the dragon is defeated in chapter 12, and cast from heaven; however, it returns again, only to be bound in the bottomless pit in chapter 20. Then, still later, it is released from the pit for a while before being cast into a "lake of fire and sulfur" (20:10). Similarly, we see that in chapter 15 the martyrs beside the glassy sea "had conquered the beast and its image and the number of its name" (15:2). However, the beast seems quite well in chapter 17, where it carries the whore of Babylon; it then is thrown into the lake of fire in chapter 19 (where it is joined by the dragon).

This back-and-forth is part of the rhythm of the book of Revelation, and must have resonated with the communities to which it was written. Evidence about the political situation in Asia Minor at the end of the first century shows that persecution was sporadic and scattered; no official, widespread, organized persecution of Christians took place until the middle of the third century CE. However, local persecution happened, and certainly the demands of Domitian to be called "Lord and God" (if indeed Revelation comes from his reign) must have been perceived as an affront to the faith of John's community. So, it would not be surprising that the dragon and the beasts appear, disappear, and appear again; they seem defeated but then are on the ascendency again, or perhaps are perceived as both at the same time. These creatures, then, allude to a complex, but ultimately antagonistic, relationship with Roman power. Their final destruction does not come easily, or in a rapid, linear fashion, but John's vision offers his reader the assurance that their destruction will finally come.

The final vision in the apocalypse affirms John's basic themes of comfort, new life, and the enduring power of God to overcome the current powers of the world. Two images stand out as most significant here. First, John repeatedly refers to water. After the final defeat of the dragon in chapter 20, the sea "gave up the dead that were in it" and "was no more" (20:13; 21:1); it is replaced by a "river of the water of life, bright as crystal, flowing from the throne of God and of the Lamb" (22:1). To the casual reader, these images may seem unimportant or simply odd: why would the sea disappear? However, the sea (and the sea dragon, discussed above) is a key image for the forces opposed to God's power throughout the Jewish and Christian tradition. It alludes to how the sea must be held back in order to create the world in Genesis 1; the sea must be parted to free the Israelites from Egypt in Exodus 14; and it is the symbol of death in Paul's explanation of baptism (Rom. 6:4). To say the sea gives up its dead and is no more expresses best the victory of God over death. John has taken the audience back to creation after the end of evil on this earth. From that point on, only the water of life is allowed.

A second critical image is of the Holy City, the New Jerusalem. As in the gospel of Mark and 2 Baruch, the New Jerusalem is central to the new creation. John describes the city

> THE NEW JERUSALEM IS CENTRAL TO THE NEW CREATION. JOHN DESCRIBES THE CITY AS ORIGINALLY HEAVENLY, AND AT THE CREATION OF THE NEW EARTH IT COMES DOWN FROM HEAVEN.

as originally heavenly, and at the creation of the new earth it comes "down out of heaven from God, prepared as a bride adorned for her husband" (Rev. 21:2). The Holy City has symbolically perfect dimensions: 12 thousand stadia around, with a wall of twelve by twelve cubits, encrusted with twelve jewels and marked by twelve pearl gates (21:11–21), as measured by the angel who accompanies John. And, in a language that speaks of a complete end to oppression, "its gates will never be shut by day" (21:25) since no foreign power will oppose it. Interestingly, however, the new Jerusalem lacks something significant: there is "no temple in the city, for its temple is the Lord God the Almighty and the Lamb" (21:22). The presence of God is pervasive in the new Jerusalem, such that no temple or priesthood is necessary to perform worship. Instead, God rules from a throne in the middle of town which flows with life-giving water, and "the home of God is among mortals" (21:3). This last characteristic of the Holy City is very important. So many people and groups today believe the building of a new temple in Jerusalem by human hands is somehow necessary for the end to come. But that is not what the book of Revelation actually says. Here in the new heaven and the new earth, the temple plays no role.

The destruction of the sea and the descent of a perfect Jerusalem clearly offer the hope against fear that John mentions at the beginning of the book of Revelation. Tragically, John's vision was often misrepresented in later interpretations and continues to be misrepresented today. Some religious leaders attempt to scare their followers and other "believers" with fear of destruction. True, the visions of Revelation are often terrifying, and we ought not downplay the appearance of violence in this text. However, by reading Revelation as a series of repeating, relatable images with underlying feelings of hope, comfort, and resistance to power, we can hope to avoid similar misinterpretations and see more clearly why those who radicalized the text ultimately failed to understand it.

This does not even begin to scratch the surface of the apocalyptic texts. Even though they are interesting and entertaining, we didn't get a chance to discuss things like the Apocalypses of Abraham or Adam, The Testament of the Twelve Patriarchs, or the Sibylline Oracles from Jewish tradition. From Christian circles, we simply don't have the space to include Shepherd of Hermas, or the Apocalypses of Paul, Peter, or Thomas, just to name a few. For this book it is most important to provide examples of how apocalyptic literature developed, how it functioned in the lives of readers and hearers, and what lasting features came to be associated with the genre. By going over the basics, we can better discuss the ways in which later interpreters mined this tradition—for better and (often) for worse.

WHEN IS THE DATE OF THE END?

I**n this second section of the book, we are going to look at sixteen failed apocalyptic predictions—some you may know about; others you might not. These predictions span the time from immediately following the period for the New Testament through the modern day. I include two predictions from what was still the ancient world, Bar Kochba and Montanism. Four spring from Europe during the Middle Ages and Reformation: Sefer Zerubbabel; Year 1000 predictions; Pope Innocent's call to crusade; and the predictions of Hans Hut. Three more come from early American history: the Shakers, the Millerites, and the Jehovah's Witnesses. The final and longest grouping is of recent apocalyptic predictions, many of which combine aspects of many other apocalyptic movements or build off popular culture. These include the apocalyptic predictions of Jonestown, Hal Lindsey, David Koresh, the Flying Saucer Apocalypses, Y2K, Harold Camping, and the Maya 2012 event.

While the predictions are diverse, they are united by a few key features:

1. The predictions come from Jewish or Christian prophets, or draw heavily on Judeo-Christian ideas of apocalypses, messianism, or a linear view of time.

2. The predictions pinpoint a moment—whether a day, or a few dates, or even a year—for the end. The predictions failed in some or all respects to materialize at the appointed hour.

It is more than just amusing or entertaining to look at what the title calls guesses, goofs, and failures. We need to answer the questions "What was it?" and "What was the consequence of the failure?" The first question allows us to get an overview of the key players, events, and methods of interpretation that contributed to each failed prediction. The second gives us an opportunity to see the negative impact prophetic failures have on the followers and for the society at large. If we are going to avoid the mistakes of the past, we have to understand where things went wrong.

THE BAR KOCHBA REVOLT

WHAT WAS IT?

The Bar Kochba revolt, or the Second Jewish Revolt, lasted from 132–135 CE. We looked at the First Jewish Revolt that led to the sacking and destruction of the temple in 70 in part one. This Jewish uprising once again featured Rome as the primary adversary. Hadrian, the Roman emperor, is said to have caused the revolt by forbidding circumcision or perhaps by insisting that a new city be built on Jerusalem's ruins. Some rabbinic traditions even hold that Hadrian told the Jewish people he would build a third temple and then immediately rescinded the deal, leading to the uprising. These changes would have felt like those instituted by Antiochus during the period of the Maccabees.

Whatever caused the revolt, Simon ben Kosiba led some among the Jewish population in Judea to go to war against Rome. Simon was known by several titles, for which we have evidence in both legend and on coins. One, from which the revolt derives its name, was Bar Kochba, which means "son of a star." This designation likely relates to the so-called "star prophecy" in Numbers 24:17: "A star shall come out of Jacob, and a scepter shall rise out of Israel." By the time of the Second Jewish Revolt, this text was widely seen as predicting a messianic leader who would save the people from the intolerance and oppression by Rome.

Simon was successful in driving the Romans from a small portion of Judea for three years (132–135 CE). Coins minted during the period when Simon was able to maintain control included the even more common title Simon adopted for himself: *nasi*. Nasi means "prince" or "ruler," but it also had messianic implications alluded to in the book of Ezekiel where the Davidic ruler is promised as a "prince forever" (37:25).

Finally, in rabbinic sources Rabbi Akiva is said to have seen Simon and called out, "This is the king Messiah!" However, evidence for Akiva's support of the revolt is mixed, and the text in which this tradition is found has the other rabbis roundly denouncing any association between Simon and the messiah to come.

There is no doubt, however, that at least some of the revolutionaries who supported him saw Bar Kochba as their liberator who would usher in a new Davidic kingdom and a new age of self-rule. Not only did the coins bear Simon's name, and the title nasi, but they also included the phrase "for the freedom of Jerusalem" along with an image of the Temple. When taken together, these words and images are a solid reminder of what the Jewish messiah was expected to do.

As we noted, Simon did experience a certain degree of success. He and his revolutionaries set up an independent seat of government in Betar, which lasted nearly three years, and letters from his own hand, discovered in the 1960s, attest to Bar Kochba's firm, military-style leadership of the area. Apparently, the achievements of the revolutionaries were troublesome enough to force Hadrian to take serious steps to regain control. He called back his top generals, among them Julius Severus, governor of Britain, to help quell the rebellion. Cassius Dio, a Roman historian writing a century later, claims that this campaign against the Jews destroyed 985 villages and killed 580 thousand Jewish people (69.14.3). Simon himself was killed in the siege at Betar. Following this revolt, Hadrian changed the name of Jerusalem to Colonia Aelia Capitolina, built a temple to Jupiter on the temple mount, and forbade any Jewish person to set foot in the city. The rebellion was entirely subdued, and messianic hopes in Bar Kochba were crushed.

For an apocalyptic failure, the Bar Kochba revolt may be the closest thing we see to a success. Bar Kochba did briefly accomplish many things associated with the messianic king imagined by Jewish apocalyptic thinkers: he arrived at a moment of crisis, he drove out the Roman occupying force, he established himself as ruler, and he ruled mindful of the religious standards of Judaism. Ultimately, however, the failure of the Bar Kochba revolt to bring about the apocalypse can be traced to the incredible might of the Roman army. Rome had already brutally suppressed a previous revolt, and it was no less vicious in subduing this second attempt.

WHAT WERE THE CONSEQUENCES OF THE FAILURE?

One consequence of the revolt is obvious: the loss of Jerusalem. After Hadrian's decree, Jews were sent into the diaspora.

The diaspora is the dispersion of Jewish people outside of the Holy Land. After the Bar Kochba revolt, Jews were not allowed to return to Jerusalem and instead migrated to other parts of the Mediterranean world, a condition which lasted for much of the next two millennia.

Centers of Judaism still flourished in North Africa and elsewhere, but the holy city was lost to paganism for several hundred years. Certainly this must have been a colossal theological crisis for the Jewish people, nearly on par with the destruction of the temple sixty years prior. Being in diaspora transformed Judaism in practice and in emphasis.

Among the most significant consequences of this failed apocalypse for Judaism was the dampening of messianic expectation among the rabbis. So thorough was the disappointment that, for some time to come, apocalyptic fervor would be suppressed and belittled in these circles. For example, in midrash (rabbinic commentary on Jewish life and Scripture), which was written after the revolt, Simon is called Bar Koziba, which means "son of a lie." Even the pronouncement of the great Rabbi Akiva that Simon was "king messiah" is followed in the midrash by this barb from Rabbi Yochanan ben Torta: "Akiva, grass will grow in your cheeks and he [the messiah] will still not have come!" It appears that the massive disappointment and the huge casualties of this failed rebellion pushed ideas of a messianic age far into the future for a while, at least among the rabbinic Jewish communities which produced midrash.

MONTANISM

WHAT WAS IT?

Montanism was a sect of Christianity that originated in the late second century CE, perhaps around 170. Montanus, from whom the movement received its name, and two prophetesses, Maximilla and Priscilla, favored a form of Christianity in which direction for the community came from prophetic utterances and visions, often received in states of ecstasy. The founders called themselves "The Three" and saw themselves as inheritors of a tradition stemming back to the daughters of Phillip the Evangelist (Acts 21:8–9). The members believed themselves "spiritual Christians," to emphasize the role of the Spirit or Paraclete in the sect and to oppose the orthodox Christians they saw as too earthly; the adherents of this sect were also known as the "New Prophecy" movement.

The Paraclete (or "Comforter," from the book of John) was central to Montanist beliefs, and there is evidence that Montanus himself embodied this role early in the movement. According to Didymus, a fourth century church historian, Montanus once said, "I am the Father, the Word, and the Paraclete" (*De Trinitate* 3.41). That is, Montanus seemed to view himself as a channel through which the Spirit of God communicated with believers (although by no means the only one). The Paraclete is a unique feature of the Gospel of John; in the gospel, it was given only to insiders (disciples) who knew the secret teaching of Jesus (see John 14). Given this association, it seems that the members of the Montanist movement saw themselves as a sort of "insider" sect of Christianity.

> MONTANUS SEEMED TO VIEW HIMSELF AS A CHANNEL THROUGH WHICH THE SPIRIT OF GOD COMMUNICATED WITH BELIEVERS.

Anti-heretical writers, of which there were many, feared Montanism's rejection of church authority in favor of individual revelation, as well as the intense asceticism of the group and their inclusion of women in positions of authority. Montanists affirmed that anyone could have prophetic gifts and that the developing orthodox church hierarchy did not limit the work and authority of the Spirit of God. Particularly, Montanist groups attracted women who found Christianity increasingly masculine and hierarchical. Indeed, many ancient writers noted the presence of women leaders among the Montanist believers, a phenomenon that was becoming less common in what became orthodox Christianity. These same anti-heretical writers often criticized the fact that women in leadership were encouraged to leave their husbands (as had Priscilla and Maximilla) and not to remarry. The focus on celibacy was related to a broadly ascetic lifestyle among the believers, based on their strong conviction that the end of the world was fast approaching and earthly pleasures ought to be avoided.

Montanism developed first in Phrygia in Asia Minor. Phrygia was already known for a particularly charismatic style of local pagan religion, and the Montanist practice seems to have meshed well with this indigenous style of worship. The movement spread throughout the Mediterranean over the next several decades, but in spite of this widespread acceptance, Phrygia remained central to the movement. Montanists (especially in the first generation) believed that the New Jerusalem of the apocalypse would descend from heaven and land in the village of Pepuza, and that this would happen at the second coming of Christ, which Montanists believed would occur in the lifetime of the current generation. According to ancient historians, members were encouraged to wait in the village for the descent of the Holy City, fasting and abandoning all earthly endeavors. The inclusion of a New Jerusalem in their theology of the end of the world indicates the community was familiar with the tradition in Revelation that the new heavenly city of Jerusalem would descend after the total defeat of evil.

Montanism was successful in gaining many converts attracted to its more democratic and charismatic style that focused on supposed direct revelations from God. Focus on individual, direct revelation from God appealed to people living at a time when orthodox Christianity was moving toward establishment and a fixed set of texts and practices. Among the most famous people to join Montanism was Tertullian, one of the church fathers who had a reputation for defending orthodoxy prior to his joining the sect in 207 CE. He, along with others, was drawn to the emphasis in this movement on direct revelation and the immediacy of the apocalypse, which encouraged believers to practice austerity and wait expectantly.

The church fathers were a group of bishops, theologians, and teachers who were concerned with identifying and protecting what they believed to be the correct (or orthodox) beliefs for Christians. They were active from the second to the seventh centuries CE and included men like Irenaeus, Tertullian, John Chrysostom, Origen, and Augustine.

However, the New Jerusalem did not arrive in Pepuza as Montanus had imagined. Tertullian, a generation later, was still expectant that the end was at hand, but within a few genera-tions more it appears that the apocalyptic fire went out of the movement, leaving only the asceticism of earlier times. By 550, Montanism disappeared entirely.

Montanism rose and fell at a time when the church was moving toward structure. Only seventy-five years after the book of Revelation, orthodox Christianity had already lost much of its orientation toward revelation, anticipation, and direct expe-rience of the Spirit of God. This was to be expected, as the apocalypse failed to come, the generations that had anticipated it in their lifetimes died out, and survival of the faith depended more and more on lasting structures that would perpetuate the beliefs of the church into the future. Montanism challenged all of this; believers could experience the power of God directly and viscerally, authority was not dependent on cultural hier-archies like gender, and an expectation of the immediate end freed believers from the need to continue anything.

Such direct access made Montanism appealing, but it also made the movement threatening to the growing orthodox strain in Christianity. Many defenders of orthodoxy com-mented on its perceived excesses and lack of decorum; others distanced themselves from the spiritual democratization that allowed individuals such control within the movement. Even-tually, the Montanist focus on charisma was lost in the con-tinuing development of Christianity in Europe.

WHAT WERE THE CONSEQUENCES OF THE FAILURE?

The Montanist challenge to orthodoxy was, finally, a challenge that could not be sustained. When the apocalypse failed to come as hoped, Montanism became a mirror of orthodoxy in many ways, only with more rigorous community standards. As Boer notes, "It [Montanism] was not very different from the stricter groups within the Catholic Church; as a result, there did not remain a strong reason for the continued existence of the Montanist church" (64–65). Unlike many of the movements we will encounter, Montanism didn't end cataclysmically; instead, it slowly lost its footing and eventually disappeared entirely from the spectrum of Christian traditions.

SEFER ZERUBBABEL AND THE CONTINUATION OF JEWISH APOCALYPTICISM

WHAT WAS IT?

The defeat of Bar Kochba in the 160s CE was, for many rabbinic writers in the intervening few centuries, a sign that the advent of the messiah was not imminent, or at least ought not to be the central focus of rabbinic discussion. However, Jewish apocalyptic imagination did not disappear entirely. A great example of the continued (or perhaps renewed) interest in a coming Messiah is a piece of Jewish apocalyptic writing called *Sefer Zerubbabel. Sefer Zerubbabel* was likely written in the seventh century CE, at a time of conflict between Byzantium Christians and Persia.

Sefer Zerubbabel looks very much like the more ancient apocalyptic literature we explored in an earlier section. It centers on the fantastic vision of Zerubbabel, a figure from the post-exilic period (before the rebuilding of the temple), possibly the same as is mentioned in Ezra 2:2 and Nehemiah 7:7. In his vision Zerubbabel is transported by means of heavenly wind to Nineveh, which the reader learns is actually Rome. Because the text was written during the period when Byzantium was a religious center of the church, it is likely that Rome actually refers to its capital—Constantinople. There, he meets the messiah, who has been held prisoner by Rome, and asks him when the deliverance of Israel will be. The angel Michael, also called Metatron, then appears and responds to Zerubbabel that many things must take place, including the destruction of the second temple and another 990 years, after which "the deliverance of the Lord will take place . . . to redeem them and to gather them by means of the Lord's Messiah" (quoted in Reeves 56).

Deliverance will come from some unusual corners in *Sefer Zerubbabel*. The Davidic messiah will be called Menachem ben Amiel. His mother Hephsibah will fight and kill two evil kings with a rod of almond wood. Five years after she has defeated them, the "Lord's Messiah," named Nehemiah ben Hushiel, will appear and gather all Israel together, but will be attacked. At this time Hephsibah will once again go into battle against the Persian army. Then, the son of Satan and his wife (represented by a beautiful statue) will have a son, called Armilos, and their son will kill Nehemiah ben Hushiel; following this, Hephsibah will again defend the people from attack. Finally, Menachem ben Amiel will return (though the elders will not recognize him) and he, a resurrected Nehemiah ben Hushiel, and Elijah will judge the nations. Sacrifice will resume in Jerusalem, and the heavenly temple will descend.

The Sefer continues with more battles, additional details of the judgment, and a much lengthier description of the character and acts of Armilos. Some suggest that the Sefer is a combination of originally different stories that were later combined. They base this on the fact that names alternate between Michael and Metatron and many events and ideas are often repeated (Himmelfarb 222). Regardless, the features of traditional apocalypses appear throughout the book:

- 💣 It uses a great figure from the past, who receives a vision.

- 💣 It "predicts" events which have already happened at the time of writing (in this case the destruction of the second temple) to lend credence and authority to the text.

- 💣 It utilizes a heavenly mediator to explain the main character's visions.

- 💣 It looks forward to a soon-to-come messianic age and the judgment of the righteous and unrighteous.

Sefer Zerubbabel also seems to have continued the apocalyptic tradition of slyly commenting on current events and criticizing current practices. Setting the revelation in Nineveh, which is also Rome in the text, is a way of speaking to the violence of Constantinople by associating that capital of Byzantium with evil empires of the past. Perhaps the most harsh condemnation against Christianity in the text is that the main adversary of the messiah is the son of Satan and a beautiful female statue, who is clearly intended to represent Byzantine icons of the Virgin.

The failed apocalyptic prediction here, that the reign of the messiah would come 990 years after the second temple, would have placed the event around 1058 CE if we count from the date of the fall. From this (and given the tendency of apocalypses to place the critical events of history in the lifetime of the writer), some have argued that *Sefer Zerubbabel* is actually an eleventh-century document. However, others have suggested the count of 990 years be started at the beginning of the second temple period, according to rabbinic understanding. That would place the date around 638 CE. In either case the messiahs who were expected in *Sefer Zerubbabel* did not ascend with Elijah to judge the dead and restore the Holy City.

WHAT WERE THE CONSEQUENCES OF THE FAILURE?

The consequences of the actual failed prediction are unknown. Apocalyptic thought did not disappear from Judaism after *Sefer Zerubbabel*, as we have several subsequent examples of apocalyptic-style literature in Judaism after this event. (For example, many Lubavitch Jews in the 1950s and after claimed that Rabbi Menachem Mendel Schneerson was in fact the messiah of the Jewish people.)

Lubavitch Judaism is a form of Jewish mysticism that originated in Europe in the eighteenth century CE. Adherents follow the teaching of seven rabbis in matters of personal piety and dedication to bringing the messianic age.

However, with this potential for apocalypticism in mind, and even in light of continued persecution from Christian and Muslim forces, Jewish writers remained wary of over-enthusiastic predictions of the end throughout the Middle Ages. Rabbi Jonathan pronounced, "Perish all those that calculate the end" (Landes 435). Many of the remaining prophetic failures would be from Christian sources or would be the result of syncretism between Christianity and other religious beliefs.

Syncretism is a mixing of beliefs between two religions. It often occurs as religions spread into new areas and encounter beliefs that are already present. To make the "new" religion palatable to the people in these areas, proponents will often take some of the old and incorporate it into the new. For example, when Christianity spread into Europe, it incorporated local practices (such as mid-winter festivals) into its own traditions, which is why Christians now celebrate Christmas in December.

Again, this is not to say that there were no Jewish apocalyptic movements in the centuries to come, but simply that the predictions of a definitive date for the end of the world occurred primarily among Christian and Christian-influenced communities.

YEAR 1000 "PREDICTIONS"

WHAT WAS IT?

Given the intensity of public interest and apocalyptic speculation prior to the year 2000, it seems almost a given that similar fear and fascination with the end of the world occurred over the year 1000 in Europe. However, the evidence is not exactly clear as to whether the end of the first millennium of Christianity instilled believers with the same intensity of fear and desire for self-preservation that the Y2K "crisis" did. In this section, we will change things up a bit. Rather than look at a clear prediction, and what befell those who believed it, we will investigate some of the arguments as to whether there was fear surrounding the approach of Y1K.

Remember the turn of 1000 was closer in time to some of the earliest church fathers than it was to some of the biblical texts themselves. One such church father was Augustine, a bishop in North Africa who lived in the fourth and fifth centuries of the Christian era. His writings provide a model for understanding the apocalyptic thought during the tenth and eleventh centuries. Augustine is perhaps the best-known biblical interpreter in the history of Christianity; his ideas about such things as "original sin" have been accepted as orthodoxy by Western Christians for centuries. Augustine professed a symbolic interpretation of the Revelation, particularly of the millennial reign of Christ, in his classic work *The City of God*. He saw the use of the number 1000 (a millennium) as a symbol for perfection and completion instead of a literal time frame. He stated:

> [God] used the thousand years as an equivalent for the whole duration of this world, employing the number of perfection to mark the fullness of time. For a thousand is the cube of ten. For ten times ten makes a hundred, that is, the square on a plane superficies. But to give this superficies height, and make it a cube, the hundred is again multiplied by ten, which gives a thousand. (*City* 20.7)

Furthermore, Augustine believed that the millennial reign of Christ and the saints in Revelation 20 was a metaphor for speaking about present realities, namely the establishment of the church on earth—and not future events.

> The devil, then, *is bound and shut up* in the abyss that he may not seduce the nations from which the Church is gathered, and which he formerly seduced before the Church existed. (*City* 20.7, emphasis mine)

Augustine expressed what we call today an amillennial belief. That means he believed that the thousand-year reign was not a literal component of the end of time. This belief that the millennium was not a literal period of time dominated Christian interpretation for hundreds of years.

★

> Amillennial is from Latin. It means not millennial. In other
> words, not one thousand literal years.

This belief steadfastly refused to see the millennium as anything other than an expression of the present church and the presence of the Spirit in all believers. That means the kingdom of God is in all believers always. The number was metaphorical, and the reign was spiritual in the here-and-now. However, as the end of the first thousand years of the Christian era approached, it appeared some Christians considered other approaches to understanding the millennial reign of Christ.

As mentioned, scholars are divided on what might have changed as the year 1000 approached. Certainly, there is some evidence that as the year approached people feared a true apocalyptic event. Consider the writings of a French monk named Ralph Glaber, at about the year 995:

> And because, in fulfillment (as we see) of the Apostle's prophecy, love waxes cold and iniquity abounds among men that are lovers of their own selves, therefore these things aforesaid befell more frequently than usual in all parts of the world about the thousandth year after the birth of our Lord and Savior. (655)

Glaber writes about a non-spiritualized end of the world and connects it with current events ("inequity abounds") as well as a period of one thousand years from the time of the life of Jesus. This seems to indicate that—in some circles at least—the millennium was understood to mark the coming of an apocalyptic event. Later, Glaber reports that "a great flocking together of people [came] to Jerusalem, unheard of in previous centuries," citing it as a sign of the coming Antichrist (quoted in McGinn 90). Similarly, sermons of the Anglo-Saxon bishop Wulfstan delivered around this time are certainly full of apocalyptic flavor, connecting current events with signs of the end of the world. And, reflecting on his earlier life in Paris, Abbo of Fleury notes that a preacher there was inciting a crowd to look for the Antichrist to come after "the number of a thousand years was completed" (quoted in McGinn 89).

However, these sermons and writings may not necessarily indicate that millennial fever was rampant. They may have been localized or unique to the person. There is a possibility that at least some of these predictions were unrelated to the year at all. For example, it is possible that Wulfstan's sermons are more immediately preoccupied with Viking invasions than with a date on the calendar (Frassetto 42). In the end, it remains possible that many of the year 1000 predictions and descriptions may not bear any relation to the year 1000 at all.

Arguments against attributing special apocalyptic meaning to the year 1000 are many, but the most obvious is calendrical. The idea of a "year 1000" is dependent on a "year 1," in this case year 1 *anno domini*, or the Year of Our Lord. This system of dating the world was developed by a monk named Dionysius Exiguus in the sixth century of the Christian era. However, it was not widely accepted as a way of organizing time, particularly around the fringes of the western empire and in the East, even by the turning of the millennium (Thompson 54). It may have been understood and accepted by monks and church officials, of course, but it is difficult to know for certain to what extent the common person knew, or even cared, about the approach of the new millennium. Further, while writers like Glaber and Wulfstan saw signs of the end all around them, the official position of the church remained Augustinian. Monks were forbidden to speculate on a date for the end, and "for a cleric to have dwelt on the eschatological significance of the date 1000 would have been foolhardy and even dangerous" (Thompson 44). And Abbo, when confronted with the apocalyptic preacher, "opposed this sermon with what force [he] could from passages in the Gospels, Revelation, and the Book of Daniel" (quoted in McGinn 89).

WHAT WERE THE CONSEQUENCES OF THE FAILURE?

Was it widely and publicly predicted that the year 1000 would be an apocalyptic year or not? There is no clear answer. While we can find examples of apocalyptic thought, it is often difficult to determine if these instances are specifically related to the date of the millennium, or whether there was a general sense of expectation or concern. Certainly, the idea that there was an apocalyptic "terror" that gripped the Christian world overstates the case. However, it would be equally wrong to say that the year 1000 was "just another year" to all Christians. The arguments as to the significance of the year have been sketched out in numerous books, and most historians advocate a middle position between the extremes.

It is enough to note here that some folks in Medieval Europe—if not all, or even the majority—connected the millennial imagery in Revelation 20 with the current times. Even further, these interpreters strayed from the dominant Augustinian amillennialist model to suggest that perhaps the 1000-year reign was somehow bound by history. This idea (amplified rather a lot) reappears often in other movements that followed, particularly in the writings of premillennialist groups such as dispensationalists.

POPE INNOCENT III AND THE CRUSADES

WHAT WAS IT?

By the thirteenth century, Christianity was a religion at war. It was at war with itself; the Roman Catholic and Orthodox branches had split over theological and structural differences, and their leaders even excommunicated each other in 1054. It was at war with powerful groups trying to gain control of Europe; Mongol invasions, for example, were relentless and successful in taking parts of Eastern Europe and the Middle East during the thirteenth century. During the period known as the Crusades, Christianity was at war with its Abrahamic neighbors; Jews were expelled from England in 1290, and Christians were into their second century of fighting against Muslims in a series of battles to regain access to Jerusalem.

It may seem unthinkable to us that the people of the Prince of Peace could be so fully engaged in war. However, at the time, the power of the Catholic Church in both the religious and political lives of Europeans was nearly absolute, and the pope's call to fight was an appeal to both heavenly and earthly power. Pope Urban II appealed to both types of authority when, at the Council of Clermont, he called for the First Crusade in 1095. Military personnel, priests, and common folks all marched off to war in order to protect Christian sites in Jerusalem, to turn back the invading Turks, and to gain both eternal and temporal rewards. Pope Urban II had promised at Clermont both pardon of sin and possible landownership to those who went out to fight. Urban II's speech launched the First Crusade, and many, many more were to follow.

We have seen repeatedly how apocalypticism addresses both religious and political issues and, given the political and religious aims of the Crusades, it is no surprise that the wars were often cloaked by apocalyptic language. Urban II, for example, employed language from the Book of Daniel to urge believers into the First Crusade:

> According to Daniel and Jerome, the interpreter of Daniel, he is to fix his tents on the Mount of Olives; and it is certain, for the apostle teaches it, that he will sit at Jerusalem in the Temple of the Lord, as though he were God. And according to the same prophet, he will first kill three kings of Egypt, Africa, and Ethiopia, without doubt for their Christian faith: This, indeed, could not at all be done unless Christianity was established where now is paganism. (Krey 36)

This kind of interpretation of Scripture, predictive reinterpretation, is common among apocalyptic prophets. That is, for many interpreters the text cited is manipulated to address a

situation during the interpreter's time. For Urban II, the Danielic vision of the desolating sacrilege was a vision of Muslim
control of Jerusalem in his own day, and thus a call to arms.

Perhaps the most interesting example of this type of reinterpretation during the Crusades, and certainly one that comes
closest to pinpointing an actual date for the end, comes from
Pope Innocent III. Innocent III had a hand in promoting three
Crusades—the Fourth, the Albigensian, and the Fifth—and was
tacitly in support of another, the ill-fated Children's Crusade.
He was the leader of Catholicism in the turbulent thirteenth
century discussed above. In April 1213, in his call for the Fifth
Crusade, Innocent issued a papal decree entitled *Quia Major*.
The bull declared that those who participated in the Crusade,
as well as those who financially contributed, would receive an
indulgence—forgiveness of sins and a reduction of time spent
in purgatory, the place or state of purification after death that
eventually allows a person access to heaven, in Catholic belief.
It also gave the reason that such a crusade—and such a massive reward—was important at that moment:

> A certain son of perdition, Muhammad the pseudo-prophet,
> arose. Through worldly enticements and carnal delights
> he seduced many people away from the truth. His perfidy
> has prospered until this day. Yet we trust in God, who has
> already given us a good omen that the end of this beast is
> drawing near. The number [of the beast], according to the
> Apocalypse of John, is 666, of which already almost six hun-
> dred years have been completed. (quoted in Tolan 194)

Innocent's interpretation of the Revelation (the Apocalypse of John) begins by asserting that the founder of Islam, Muhammad, is the beast of the Revelation. This in itself is not too unusual; people have often interpreted the image of the beast as a religious or political opponent. But then, Innocent takes the number of the beast and uses it not as a code for a name (since he asserts he already knows who the beast is) but as a marker of years. He asserts instead that the 666 refers to the time from the beginnings of Islam to its end, and that nearly six hundred of the allotted years have already passed. This leaves some wiggle room as to the actual predicted year of the end, since it is unclear when Innocent started his count. However, with the declaration that they were almost six hundred years in, and with the reminder that the bull was written in 1213, it certainly appears that Innocent expected the apocalypse to arrive by the end of the 1280s.

WHAT WERE THE CONSEQUENCES OF THE FAILURE?

Innocent's claim that the apocalypse was coming was intended to inspire potential Crusaders. By tying the call to war to cosmic events, the pope hoped to convince those who fought (and those who sent money) that they were participating in something greater than themselves and something destined to succeed. The Crusaders had, until this point, been only moderately successful in the goal of retaining Christian sacred sites; mostly they faced loss after loss to the Muslims. People found the losses confusing and theologically disturbing; as the Crusades wore on, the need to understand and interpret the constant defeats became central to the work the church believed it needed to do. Thus, Innocent III reached for a key apocalyptic ideal: that a righting of the scales of justice was delayed for only a little longer.

Innocent died before the Fifth Crusade was underway; his successor, Pope Honorius III, continued the preparations. The apocalyptic style the church used to rally Crusaders to fight worked, but the efforts did not bring about victory. The apocalypse did not come, for one thing, but the Crusade itself was not directed primarily at protecting sites like Jerusalem that were associated with apocalyptic visions or biblical history. Instead, most of the major conflicts were in Egypt, perhaps under the belief that an attack on this Muslim stronghold would weaken their power over Palestine. Crusader victories were overturned shortly thereafter, and crusading continued through the next fifty years. Ultimately, all that was accomplished was a worsening of relations between Christians, Jews, and Muslims. The results of the conflicts can still be seen today in the castles and landmarks that appear throughout the Middle East.

HANS HUT AND THE ANABAPTISTS

WHAT WAS IT?

The Protestant Reformation in the sixteenth century was first and foremost a time of revolution against the religious authorities in Europe. At this time, religion and politics were vitally important and often closely linked such that rebellion against one seemed rebellion against the other, and, in turn, against the whole of society. The reformers differed on whether one ought to support the more political features of the revolution. Martin Luther, for example, actively sided with the political authorities in Germany against the common people, suggesting that the princes of Germany "smite, stab, and slay all the [revolutionary peasants] that you can" (quoted in Johnson 283). Others, however, contended that the spiritual revolution in Europe had a very earthly component, and that the political revolutions being fought at the time also had theological importance—even for the coming end of time.

THOMAS MUNTZER, ENCOURAGED ARMED REBELLION IN HOPES OF HURRYING THE APOCALYPSE ALONG.

Political and religious persecution of some reform groups, particularly the Anabaptists, only intensified this apocalyptic expectation. The Anabaptists rejected infant baptism and believed that none should be compelled to be part of any church. The Anabaptist movement is most closely associated with reformers like Jacob Hutter and Menno Simons (hence, members of one form of Anabaptist belief became known as Hutterites, the other Mennonites), who advocated pacifism. Others, however, such as Thomas Muntzer, encouraged armed rebellion in hopes of hurrying the apocalypse along. He and others saw the coming end as a time in which the intense persecution of Anabaptists would be set right and thus sought to bring it by force if necessary.

During this time, a book binder named Hans Hut predicted the arrival of the apocalypse by May 27, 1528, the date of Pentecost that year. Hut was an Anabaptist, and among the more radical of the movement with a strong apocalyptic expectation. There is evidence that he was quite familiar with the work, and perhaps the person, of Thomas Muntzer. Hut asserted that the apocalypse would begin with the persecution of the elect, which he believed was already occurring; then, the apocalyptic righting of the world would be carried out in series of earthly battles, in which governmental and church authorities would be slaughtered by Turkish invaders, reducing the population by a third. Hans Hut and his fellow Anabaptists would hide in the wilderness and await a time when they could emerge to finish what the "infidel" Turkish invaders had started and judge or perhaps kill the remaining authorities (Wilson 29). Then, the dead would rise and establish the reign of Christ on earth. The new heaven and new earth would be a place of abundance and would be marked with a redistribution of community goods (Packull 55). While Hut affirmed that the violent overthrow of authority would eventually involve the elect, he himself never did take up arms to accomplish this goal.

Hut did not live to see his prediction fail. He was imprisoned at Augsburg and died there on December 6, 1527. The following day, authorities bound his corpse to a chair in the courtroom and sentenced it to death by burning at the stake.

WHAT WERE THE CONSEQUENCES OF THE FAILURE?

Hut and the revolutionary Anabaptists were not the only types of Anabaptists, as previously noted. The pacifist groups, while still expecting the reign of Christ, did not seek to actively engage earthly authorities the way Muntzer and Hut had. However, the millennialist vision and more aggressive forms of the faith characterized by Hans Hut did inspire others. Among these were Jan Matthys and John Bockelson, who briefly transformed the city of Munster, Germany into a militant apocalyptic kingdom between 1533–35; Bockelson even proclaimed himself the Davidic messiah who had been foretold would rule over all the earth (Cohn 271–73). The kingdom fell at the hands of the Bishop after a brutal siege, and the millennial form of the Anabaptist faith rapidly disappeared.

The apocalyptic prediction of Hans Hut is significant in part because it was so radically this-worldly, meaning it emphasized a kingdom of God that would come in the current political system and on the earth as it was right now. For much of the post-biblical history of Christianity, the apocalypse was interpreted metaphorically in line with the writings of St. Augustine. Especially after the failure of the Montanist movement, apocalypticism had been pushed further and further beyond the daily lives of believers. However, the Protestant Reformation—itself a this-worldly movement—changed that interpretation, sometimes radically. In some ways, this imminent apocalyptic theory closely mirrors the apocalypticism of ancient Jewish and Christian texts: they, too, predicted a coming kingdom on earth, which would overthrow the powers of this world and set right the scales of justice. The most radical expressions of the Anabaptist movement saw the world much as the Sons of Light and Sons of Darkness the Qumran community had talked about in the Dead Sea Scrolls 1500 years before.

The total failure of Hut's prediction of the end of the world and the fall of the kingdom at Munster and its so-called Davidic messiah to the church did not quell completely apocalypticism and apocalyptic thought in Christianity, nor did it return the faith to a metaphorical or allegorical understanding of the apocalypse. However, it did reduce some of the intensely militaristic aspects of the apocalyptic ideology. Still, visions of the end continued. Especially as Christianity moved to the New World, Protestant groups retained the emphasis on a coming kingdom on earth; they just saw it in a New Jerusalem far from Palestine.

APOCALYPTIC THOUGHT IN AMERICA

THREE FORMS

Christian interpreters of the book of Revelation, particularly in America, offered three quite different interpretations of the thousand-year reign. So far, we discussed what is called amillennialism. This is the interpretation of the thousand years found in Augustine. According to him, the reign was not a historical time period at all, but a metaphorical and spiritual way of speaking about the age of the church. The second interpretation of the millennium is called *postmillennialism*. This is the belief that the millennium was a reality we were already living "into" as we improved the situations of the poor or committed ourselves to the betterment of society. Christians were, in a sense, already a part of the thousand-year kingdom and were in the process of moving it on to perfection. At the end of this time, Christ would come to complete the task of renewing heaven and earth.

The third way of interpreting the millennial reign of Christ is called *premillennialism*. It envisions Christ returning before the reign to save the faithful. Premillennialists do not see the church working to progressively bring the kingdom of God. Instead, they view the world as corrupt and irredeemable, so believers are not bringing about the reign of Christ but waiting for it to break into the world at some future point.

THE SHAKERS

As Christianity moved from Europe to the New World, it took a different form than it had in Europe. The United Society of Believers in Christ's Second Appearing, better known as the Shakers, was an offshoot of the Quaker movement that bridged the Old World and the New. Shakerism was a charismatic, communitarian, apocalyptic sect of Christianity that formed in England in the 1770s and moved to America shortly before the American Revolution. The Shakers existed prior to that date, but formed completely under the leadership of "Mother" Ann Lee, a gifted preacher and teacher, who claimed to have prophetic visions. In one vision, God revealed to her that at the Second Coming, Christ would return in female form, and that she was this female messiah. In the *Compendium*, compiled after Lee's death, the Shakers affirm her unique significance:

> Thus, out of the last of the "witnesses," the Quakers, the "for-ty-and-two months" having expired, arose Ann Lee and her little company, to whom Christ appeared the second time, "without sin unto salvation," and made a new revelation to her of the seven principles, and of all the truths that had been revealed, in his first appearing, to Jesus; the practice of which constituted him the first Christian Church; and the same principles being reduced to practice by Ann Lee, con-stituted her the second Christian Church. (7.10)

The idea that Ann Lee was the second appearing of Christ had significant theological and practical implications for the Shakers. Primarily, it meant that the millennium, or prophe-sized rule of Jesus Christ, had already begun. That is, no longer were humans waiting for a future date for the apocalypse; it already had begun. The *Compendium* makes this clear, with ref-erences to the "witnesses" and forty-two months from the Rev-elation "having expired." Later, in the same text, Shakers profess that the book of Revelation was impossible to understand "and could not be comprehended until the central event—the sec-ond appearing of Christ—had transpired" (9.67). In both cases, the reign of Christ is described as having begun in the past. Unlike other apocalyptic communities, the Shakers believed we were already living in the millennial kingdom described in Revelation.

One of the outgrowths of this belief was a commitment of all members to celibacy. Men and women lived separately, and sex was believed to be a sign of the fallenness of the world and the church prior to the advent of the Second Messiah (Taysom 107). Because the believers believed they were living in the end times, in the restored kingdom, sex was impermissible. It could lead one away from the "true faith" and the "true church" through impurity. Further, sex was unnecessary; since the kingdom was upon them, the procreation of future generations was pointless.

The Shakers' worship was charismatic, visionary, and enthusiastic, particularly in the United States. Like many movements that were a part of the Great Awakening, Shakerism emphasized individual salvation and individual experience of God, which they expressed physically by falling down, jerking, speaking in tongues, singing, and dancing. The community was also democratic in terms of its understanding of spiritual gifts: any member of the community could receive the Spirit of God, since all were part of the eschatological kingdom.

Another example of the Shaker belief in the here-and-now kingdom was the participation in a twice-yearly ritual eschatological banquet, an imaginary meal intended to be reminiscent of the apocalyptic feast shared by Christ and the church in the Revelation. Since the kingdom already existed in the present, the true church could share in the spiritual feast in the present as well. As Zamora states, "The meal and its attendant ceremonies reminded the Shakers that they were not of this world, but already part of the world which most thought was yet to come" (44).

The idea that the messiah had come as a woman became the reason for equality between women and men in the Shaker movement and was another defining feature of the apocalyptic kingdom they envisioned. God was conceived as both Father and Mother, so femaleness was not seen as disqualifying a woman from leadership or full participation in the community. As the *Rules* state:

> As Christ's first appearing was only to and in the male part of humanity, the Jewish as well as the Gentile Christian Churches were governed almost entirely by men. The Roman Catholic and Protestant world know only male rulers; woman is ignored. The Quakers, the last of the "witnesses," began to include the female element in their system; but not until Christ had made his second appearance in and to the female, was woman ever allowed a full and equal share in any civil or religious government, or established in the possession of her just and equal rights. (7.15)

Shakers lived out this principle of equality in their treatment of each other. Once established in America, and after Ann's death, believers lived on communal farms throughout the Eastern United States; men and women lived and worked in harmony and mutuality, and all believers shared property. Shakers practiced pacifism, like their "parent" Quaker church, and were abolitionists. At its height, Shakers had utopian communities in nearly twenty locations throughout the Northeastern United States, with a membership of about six thousand. However, after another hundred years of activity, Shaker communities began to shrink and disappear. Today, there are only a handful of Shakers in the United States, living in a community in Maine.

WHAT WAS THE CONSEQUENCE OF THE FAILURE?

The Shakers bear striking similarities to the Montanists: charismatic leadership, prophetic women, egalitarianism, and a clear sense of living at the very end of days. Like Montanists, Shaker populations simply slowly declined over an extended period of time. The decline of the Shakers can be attributed to several factors, but certainly the commitment to celibacy is one very important reason. Changes in the American culture, particularly the failure of other utopian groups and the pessimism following a century of war, also likely contributed to the decline. However, given the different perspective of the Shakers—particularly their belief that the messiah had come and they were living in the kingdom—it is difficult to call the messianic claims of Ann Lee "failed." Unlike communities that point to a specific day in the future, and then are disappointed when the cataclysm does not arrive on schedule, the Shakers pointed to the present and to the past. Shakers believed throughout their existence—and to this day—that the apocalypse has arrived and the kingdom is a present reality in our midst.

THE MILLERITES

WHAT WAS IT?

Perhaps more than any other apocalyptic prediction in America, the Millerites are synonymous with failed end-times prophecy and its consequences. William Miller's predictions of the coming of Christ in 1843 and 1844 were widespread and apparently quite widely believed. When Christ did not come to reclaim the faithful from their hilltops, the event became known as The Great Disappointment.

William Miller was a native of New York who became intrigued by the apocalyptic literature in Daniel and the book of Revelation, believing the texts predicted a coming end of days. Miller had a premillennialist view, that is, he believed that the faithful would be raptured into heaven prior to the thousand-year reign of Christ described in Revelation, and that this date had not yet come but was still in the future. (This is opposed to postmillennialist thinkers, who believed that the reign of Christ, while a literal event, had already begun at some point in the church's past.) Miller was eager to use the Scriptures to point to a date when the faithful would be vindicated and the dead would rise. He did so with a fascinating mix of literalism, proof-texting, and speculation, which he spelled out in his "Rules of Biblical Interpretation." In these rules, Miller asserted that only Scripture could explain other Scripture, and that by gathering as many scriptures as possible on a topic, one would find definitive answers to any subject one wished to understand. This was true, according to Miller, even if the scriptures one gathered were only indirectly related to the concern at hand.

> Proof-texting is a way of reading the Bible in which individual verses, or even parts of verses, are used to prove a point without regard for the context in which they were written.

Miller's exegesis (or method of drawing meaning from the Bible), as determined by these rules, is most evident in his famous sermons on the eschaton, or the end of the present world, later turned into books to continue and spread the message. Miller tended—as he had indicated in his rule book—to "prove" his interpretation of the Bible with strings of other passages in the Bible. In the first chapter of *Evidence from Scripture and History of the Second Coming of Christ*, for example, Miller sought to prove that the wicked would be destroyed by fire at the Second Coming by citing a chain of thirteen passages of scripture from Deuteronomy to Revelation.

> The full chain of proof-texts offered by Miller on this matter include the following: Deut. 32:22; 2 Sam. 22:9–10, 13; Ps. 97:2–3; Isa. 66:16; Dan. 7:11; Nah. 1:5, Hab. 3:3–5; Mal. 4:1; Matt. 3:12; 13:30, 40, 49; 2 Thess. 1:7–8; 2 Pet. 3:10; Rev. 18:8.

These texts all have the word *fire* in them somewhere, but there is no other discernable connector between the passages, and they certainly make no mention of fire burning the wicked at the Second Coming with the lone exception of 2 Peter, at the very end of the string of texts. Miller, however, asserted that the passages, drawn from across biblical literature and time, made the point clearly about the apocalypse to come.

Miller was particularly fascinated by the mention in Daniel 8:14 that "for two thousand three hundred evenings and mornings" the sanctuary would stay desolated, and then "shall be restored to its rightful state." It is believed that this prophetic utterance was a response to the violation of the second temple under Antiochus Epiphanes in the 160s BCE; however, Miller argued that it couldn't simply be about that time, since "[Antiochus] and his kingdom were made desolate and destroyed before Christ," and Jesus had referenced the same text as referring to Roman power centuries later (Lecture 3). To Miller, this proved that the text was not meant to be read as a literal description of days until the restoration of the second temple. Instead, one ought to take each day to mean one year, "for God hath so ordered the prophets to reckon days" (ibid.). Miller concluded that one could take each day in the text to mean one year and then do the following:

> [Count from] the going forth of the decree to build the walls of Jerusalem in troublous times, 457 years before Christ; take 457 from 2300, and it will leave A.D. 1843; or take 70 weeks of years, being 490 years, from 2300 years, and it will leave 1810 after Christ's death. Add his life, (because we begin to reckon our time at his birth,) which is 33 years, and we come to the same A.D. 1843. (ibid.)

With this logic, Miller set the date the end would come sometime between March 1843 and March 1844.

It seems that the times were particularly right for Miller's predictions to catch hold of the American imagination. As westward expansion continued, a sense of rugged individualism spread through the country; meanwhile Miller, a farmer with no formal training in biblical studies, seemed to embody the spirit that anyone could understand the Bible without any authority from a pastor or priest. Further, at the time of Miller's preaching, the country was in the midst of the Second Great Awakening, a time of religious revival and popular preaching that emphasized that everyone could be redeemed. Miller's premillennialist ideals were a clean fit with this emphasis, in that the time had not yet come and repentance was still possible before the judgment. Compounding the religious excitement of the time, an economic downturn at the end of the 1830s seems to have resulted in a lack of confidence in the government's ability to solve social problems or provide for its citizens, dampening some of the optimism of previous decades that had led to more utopian apocalyptic movements like the American Shaker communities. For some, the failure of the government was a sign that the end times must be near, and Miller himself compared contemporary governments to beasts of the apocalypse (Thompson 98–99; Lawson 210), something we have

> MILLER'S PROPHETIC GOOF LED TO PEOPLE TAUNTING HIM BY CALLING AFTER HIM, "HAVE YOU NOT GONE UP?"

seen throughout the movements covered in this book. Religious revivalism, individualism, emotionalism, and economic uncertainty merged quickly around the person and ideas of William Miller, and estimates are that as many as 50 thousand Millerites were awaiting the end by 1834 (Zamora 46).

Oddly, it was not the passing of the March 1844 date that brought the most attention, although it did result in disillusionment among a significant portion of Miller's flock and was devastating to Miller himself. Instead, when that date passed, the most devout Millerites revised their predictions to later that same year, namely to October 22, which a preacher named Samuel Snow believed was the correct time. He calculated this day because it was the Jewish Day of Atonement, relating back to the Danielic prophecy of cleansing, and called the new date the "true midnight cry." Miller himself seemed to hedge on this date, not endorsing it until a few weeks before the proposed time. In spite of his hesitance, the faithful gathered in churches and on hilltops to await the coming of Christ; when again he did not come, believers were completely devastated. "Our fondest hopes and expectations were blasted," one Millerite later wrote, "and such a spirit of weeping came over us as I never experienced before" (quoted in Boyer 81). Apparently, the Millerites were mocked heavily in the days that followed October 22 as well. Miller himself wrote to a friend of the taunting he endured, including the continual call "Have you not gone up?" (Tucker 97).

WHAT WERE THE CONSEQUENCES OF THE FAILURE?

The Great Disappointment, as the passing of the October date came to be known, had widespread repercussions throughout the American religious landscape. For one thing, it became taboo, even in premillennialist circles, to focus on specific dates for the apocalypse, for fear of again looking the fool as Miller had. Instead, a new type of premillennialism—dispensationalism, which we will discuss further—took the place of date-setting for the most conservative Protestant groups.

For the most hardcore Millerites, however, a new understanding of the date was necessary to maintain the faith in which they had invested so much. These believers claimed that the apocalypse did in fact occur in October of 1844. Hiram Edson claimed—the very next day—that the return of Christ had happened, but that it had occurred in the heavenly sanctuary where Christ had atoned for the sins of believers who had died (Tucker 98).

Ellen G. White, another Millerite, claimed that she was a prophetess and that her prophetic visions were a sign that the Parousia and reign of Christ was indeed upon us. Her followers became known as Seventh-Day Adventists, and they claimed that the 1843 date was the time at which all but one of the apocalyptic prophecies (the gathering of the 144,000) were fulfilled. A return to biblical law—such as keeping the Sabbath on Saturday—and spreading of the Adventist's beliefs would hasten the completion of this final piece, and the apocalypse would come. Interestingly, White's visions also convinced her that bodily purity was a key feature of the elect; hence, she forbade meat, alcohol, and tobacco. An Adventist follower, Dr. John Harvey Kellogg, took these words to heart and invented Corn Flakes to replace the meat-heavy breakfasts of most Americans in the late 1800s. According to Seventh-Day Adventists archives, current membership is 17,214,683 worldwide. The prophetic and millennialist aspects of the Seventh-Day Adventists will need to be revisited, for from this movement arose the sect known as the Branch Davidians in the twentieth century.

JEHOVAH'S WITNESSES

WHAT WAS IT?

The Jehovah's Witnesses are a Christian sect also known as the Watchtower Bible and Tract Society, or simply Witnesses. They are an American expression of apocalypticism, although they have now spread their apocalyptic beliefs throughout the world most famously by door-to-door evangelism. The Witnesses have much in common with the Adventist movement and, like them, famously predicted the end of the world on several occasions, notably in 1914, 1918, 1925, and 1975. They were formed under the leadership of Charles Russell in the late 1800s and continue to add to their numbers today, in spite of the apparent failure of these apocalyptic predictions.

Charles Russell (1852–1916), the founder of the Jehovah's Witness movement, was strongly influenced by the Adventist tradition. He attended Adventist services and was familiar with William Miller's premillennialist biblical interpretations. The appeal of such a premillennialist interpretation was apparently a draw for Russell. Beginning in the 1870s, he gathered a group of friends to study the Bible and attempt to understand its "predictions" of the end of the world. These investigations led him to predict that a 40-year period of judgment had begun in 1874 and that the reign of Christ would commence in 1914.

That date was chosen by means of a complex set of calculations of the length of the "Gentile period," from Luke 21:24. Jehovah's Witnesses believe that the Gentile period, when Jerusalem would be "trampled" by the nations, began in 607 BCE and would last for a period of "seven times," a number garnered from Daniel 4. This amount of time is calculated as 2,520 years (using the year-for-a-day method that Miller also used). From 607 BCE, that means that the Gentile period would end in 1914. Russell predicted that the battle of Armageddon would occur in 1914 and the end would come, probably on October 1. It would be the end of a forty-year period of Christ's invisible presence on earth and the beginning of his reign. To prepare people for the coming apocalypse, Russell began publication of a newsletter called the *Zion's Watch Tower and Herald of Christ's Presence.*

The coming of World War I was seen as the first indicator that Armageddon was just around the corner. However, when the October 1, 1914, date passed, Russell revised the prediction of the return, citing possibly 1915 or 1918. Russell was in poor health by this time, however, and died in 1916. His successor, Joseph Rutherford, argued that Russell had been right about the 1914 prediction after all. He claimed that the apocalyptic battle between Christ and Satan had occurred in that year, but it was a battle in heaven. Over time, the Witnesses began to teach that Satan had been thrown down to earth in this battle and lived here now. This meant that the earth, and particularly its religions and governments, were the abode of Satan. Therefore, Witnesses believed that the Second Coming had arrived but could not be seen. Christ was enthroned, and Armageddon was near at hand. As Rutherford famously said, "Millions now living will never die!" Later, Rutherford also began to teach that the number of the saved mentioned in the Revelation (144,000) was to be taken literally. This small flock of chosen people would rule with Christ in the kingdom, which was also perceived literally as an actual government in heaven.

The Jehovah's Witness movement continued to grow over the next decades but did not lose its millennial flavor. Several additional end-times predictions were made. Among the most famous was the prediction that Armageddon would occur in 1975. This prediction was based on the Witnesses doctrine that humanity was made in autumn of 4026 BCE. In the early 1970s, some speculated that each thousand-year period since then has been one "day," and that the end of the sixth day (six thousand years) would be the beginning of the "rest day" or millennium of God's reign. Missionary work increased among witnesses, both in the United States and across the globe, in light of the possibility that 1975 marked the end. According to Penton, in that year leading up to the predicted time, there was a nearly 10 percent growth in the number of Witnesses worldwide (99).

WHAT WERE THE CONSEQUENCES OF THE FAILURE?

When the apocalypse again failed to come for the Witnesses, the immediate consequences were quite dramatic. Within two years, membership dropped significantly (Penton 99). Disillusionment at the failure seemed to reach even the leadership of the movement. Penton notes, speaking in front of a crowd in Toronto, that Witnesses leader Fredrick Franz blamed the assembled faithful for the failure, saying, "Do you know why nothing happened in 1975? . . . It was because *you* expected something to happen" (100). Along with placing the blame on others, Franz also argued that the Watchtower Society was wrong to calculate the 6000-year period from the creation of Adam; instead, they should start the clock from the formation of Eve, and no one knew when that was (100). The Watchtower Society did not issue any sort of apology for the trauma and blame until four years later. Tactics like blaming the followers following a prophetic goof are quite common, and we will discuss them in the concluding section of the book.

Long term, however, Witnesses have rebounded from the failure, and the group continues to be successful at proselytizing, or converting, non-believers. The National Council of Churches Survey found that in 2009 alone, the Jehovah's Witnesses gained 4.7 percent in membership, the single largest gain of any denomination.

JONESTOWN

WHAT WAS IT?

Jonestown was a socialist collective community set up in the jungles of Guyana by members of the Peoples Temple, and was named after the founder and head of the Peoples Temple, Reverend Jim Jones. Beginning in the 1950s, Jones had been a preacher who claimed that he had healing and prophetic gifts. He advocated care for the poor, racial inclusivity, and gender equality in the churches he founded (first in Indiana, then in California). He also believed himself to be a manifestation of Christ; he claimed that as a messianic figure he would save many from the nuclear war that was imminent (Wessinger 33). Jones contended that this war would strike down the United States, which he called Babylon and the Antichrist because it did not follow the socialist principles he advocated. Jones first predicted the end of the world would happen on July 15, 1967, but after that date passed without incident he continued to express expectation of the end (Chidester 109–10).

Jones' personality and charisma has been discussed in many academic and popular studies of the Peoples Temple and the later Jonestown tragedy. By all accounts, Jones was a charismatic preacher and a visionary whose claims that "apostolic socialism" could be established in this world drew large crowds of optimistic believers. Members of the Jonestown community referred to him as "Dad" and claimed that he saved them from mistreatment, racism, violence, and economic disaster in the United States. They viewed the space he created in Guyana as a utopia (Smith 1117). However, claims made by critics that Jones was drug addicted, sexually manipulative with adherents, and physically abusive have been substantiated. While the full portrait of Jones has not yet been painted, what is clear is that, as the community drew closer together, and particularly after the move from the US to Guyana, Jones expected (and was given) obedience; this obedience was not to Jones only, but to the needs of the group to survive.

The Peoples Temple members grew more isolated and hostile, particularly after 1972. Members believed that journalists, racist groups, the US government, and defectors all posed a threat to their way of life (Wessinger 39). By 1973, the community had set in motion a plan to leave the United States to escape these threats, and in 1977 Jones moved the group members to Guyana to establish a collective farm, calling it "The Promised Land," away from those they believed wished to dismantle their community. The group eventually consisted of about one thousand members, many of whom were elderly or children under eighteen. While the group was in Guyana, outside pressures—especially from the anti-cult group Concerned Relatives—did not relent.

The Concerned Relatives was a group of actual relatives of Jonestown members. They organized under the leadership of Tim and Grace Stoen in 1977. The Stoen's six-year-old son, John, was being raised at Jonestown against the couple's wishes.

The community (particularly Jones himself) became more and more convinced that evil forces were attempting to disassemble the collective.

As paranoia against outsiders grew, talk in the community turned more and more to the idea of "revolutionary suicide." After the move to Guyana, other types of religious rhetoric (such as messianism, or belief in the messiah) ceased to function, and the sole emphasis was on martyrdom in the service of the group and its mission (Moore 118). This rhetoric, the isolation of the community, Jones' personal paranoia, and the community's constant fears of dismantlement played a role in justifying discussions of mass suicide. Some former members reported later that "suicide drills" took place for months before the tragedy, with members consuming beverages they believed to be poisoned as a "loyalty test" (Chidester 109–10). This loyalty was not exclusively directed toward Jones but was also a commitment to the community values and shared beliefs (Moore 119).

Following a visit from some investigators in November 1978, the Jonestown community believed they were increasingly under threat. Members of the Peoples Temple shot and killed many of the investigators at an airstrip a few miles from Jonestown as they attempted to leave. Congressman Leo Ryan, who came to investigate Jonestown, was among the dead. Shortly thereafter, Jones gathered the members of the Peoples Temple at the central pavilion. He said, in part:

> Some months I've tried to keep this thing from happening. But I now see it's the will—it's the will of Sovereign

Being that this happen to us. That we lay down our lives to protest against what's being done. That we lay down our lives to protest at what's being done. The criminality of people. The cruelty of people. . . . I just know that there's no point—there's no point to this. We are born before our time. They won't accept us. And I don't think we should sit here and take any more time for our children to be endangered. Because if they come after our children, and we give them our children, then our children will suffer forever. (Maaga 156)

As Jones' last speech makes clear, the final hours (and perhaps months) at Jonestown were marked by despair at the horrors of the world around them, fear for their children, and a desperate desire to escape the cruelty of this world. Minutes after this speech, adults fed to children, and then took themselves, a mix of tranquilizers and cyanide in fruit punch. Jones and Annie Moore, the last to die at Jonestown, died by gunshot wounds. More than nine hundred people took their own lives or were killed at the hands of family members.

WHAT WERE THE CONSEQUENCES OF THE FAILURE?

The scale of death at Jonestown has made it the classic example of apocalyptic thought gone horribly wrong. No other millennialist tragedy since has come close to the number of lives lost. The rapid movement from a collective, inclusive church to a catastrophic, deadly cult in only a few short years is deeply distressing. Despite the early potential for the Peoples Temple to become a progressive millennial movement, seeking the good of its members and striving to bring heaven on earth, the move to Guyana under duress was the final decision that destroyed that possibility (Wessinger 39). The tragedy of Jonestown exists, then, on many levels.

Early reports placed all the blame for the massive loss of life on Jones and his "brainwashing." Later studies have recognized the community members believed that suicide was the best choice for themselves and their children (see especially Maaga, *Hearing the Voices of Jonestown*). In his analysis of the event, J. Z. Smith noted the exaggerated language in media reports, op-eds, and academic studies after the discovery of the bodies. He noted the desire of many to label Jonestown a cult and play up the more bizarre aspects of life in the commune. However, Smith went on to say that Jonestown must not be characterized as some bizarre and utterly foreign expression of human life, but as an example of religious behavior that we must find a way to understand simply because it is human. The fact that the members of the community were unable to establish their utopian goals was devastating to the Peoples Temple. That devastation combined with the desire finally and ultimately to be free of the perceived oppression led to the tragedy. Making sense of Jonestown is an act of remembering that "nothing human is foreign to me" (111). And, even more importantly, understanding the reasons that Jonestown happened—particularly the isolation and oppression they felt—can help us recognize another potential tragedy before it is too late.

Regardless of whether Jones himself or the members of the community bear more responsibility for the tragedy, more than thirty years later Jonestown is a reminder not to underestimate the ways in which apocalyptic ideals such as messianism and utopianism can play out in the lives of real people.

★ HAL LINDSEY AND *THE LATE GREAT PLANET EARTH*

WHAT WAS IT?

One of the most well-known strains of premillennialism is known as premillennial dispensationalism, a position most famously espoused by John Nelson Darby in the 1820s. Darby believed there had been a series of fixed and discernable eras, or dispensations, in human history. The current age, commonly called the "church age," was the last before the end of time. At the end of this age, and prior to the calamities of the apocalypse, Jesus would return to gather the faithful into heaven, an act Darby called the rapture. It is interesting to note that Darbyite dispensationalism believed the timetable of history to be so fixed that predicting a date for the end was a complete waste of time (Thompson 101)!

Premillennial dispensationalism became a favorite understanding of the apocalyptic timeline among fundamentalist Christians in the twentieth century, promoted by the movement as a return to "literal" interpretations of Scripture. The production of the *Scofield Reference Bible* that contained footnotes based on Darby's interpretation of the millennium helped increase the popularity of premillennial dispensationalism (Frykholm 17).

A famous proponent of premillennial dispensational-ism was Harold Lee "Hal" Lindsey, who was born in 1923 in Texas. As an adult, Lindsey received his theological education at Dallas Seminary, one of the foremost centers of dispensa-tional thought. In the 1970s, 1980s, and again just prior to the year 2000, Lindsey predicted the coming end of the world in a series of New York Times bestselling books. The first was called *The Late Great Planet Earth* (1970); later, Lindsey published *1980s: Countdown to Armageddon* (1982), *The Final Battle* (1996), and *Planet Earth—2000 A.D.* (1996), among many others.

Lindsey's works do not change much about the basic dis-pensationalist mode of thinking, but his books did do three things: (1) they popularized premillennial dispensationalism on a massive scale, (2) they tied the end of the current dispen-sation to the formation of the modern state of Israel, and (3) they offered to pinpoint a date (or several dates) for the coming pre-tribulation rapture.

In *Late Great Planet Earth* Lindsey offered the first of his pre-dictions for the end. In this book, Lindsey contends that the formation of the State of Israel in 1948 was a key indicator of the coming apocalyptic age. The belief that the re-establishment of Israel is a necessary precondition of the apocalyptic return of Christ is called Christian Zionism. Citing Jesus' exhortation in the gospel of Matthew that "this generation will not pass away until all these things have taken place" (24:34) and asserting that "a generation in the Bible is something like forty years," Lindsey in essence (although not explicitly) dated the rapture to sometime in 1988 (Lindsey 54). However, Lindsey hedged his bets by noting that in Matthew and elsewhere, Jesus quotes the book of Daniel, in which the end of the "abomination of desolation" in the temple is an indicator of the apocalypse. Lindsey believed that the temple must be rebuilt in order for Jesus to return to rapture the faithful, and that the first step in doing so was to retake the temple mount. In *Late, Great* Lindsey wrote that this first step occurred in the 1967 Six-Day War and that within a "generation" the temple would be rebuilt and offerings would resume (57). Thus, if not in 1988, on the far end, the apocalypse was sure to occur by 2007.

Lindsey's subsequent books have followed much the same line, identifying current events with biblical texts and indicating that the images in these ancient scriptures refer explicitly to present realities (rather than past persecution, for example). He has been particularly interested in the potential association between the Revelation and a nuclear war. Revelation 6:14, in which "the sky vanished like a scroll . . . and every mountain and island was removed from its place" for example, is a "perfect picture of an all-out nuclear exchange" (quoted in Wojcik 44). Most books offer similarly vague and overstated connections, and all of these connections are presented as irrefutable fact, with ample graphic descriptions of devastation and death. Lindsey expresses a level of giddy enthusiasm that conflicts with his gruesome predictions as if he secretly delights in the coming destruction. This attitude has been described as an "unholy zest" (Boyer 128).

Lindsey's prediction that the 1980s would almost certainly be our last decade clearly did not pan out. Over the next decade, Lindsey continued to revise the timeline for the end, always with current events as his main touchstone. For example, in the late 1990s Lindsey suggested that true Christians shouldn't make any firm plans after the year 2000, and yet later revised these predictions to include the impending Y2K technical debacle he believed would occur on January 1 (see the discussion of Y2K for more). And, following the election of President Obama, Lindsey wrote an article for the *World News Daily* suggesting the president's popularity outside of the United States had "prepped [the] world for the Antichrist."

WHAT WERE THE CONSEQUENCES OF THE FAILURE?

Fascinatingly, Lindsey's continual failure to accurately predict the year of the end seems not to phase him or his followers. He still maintains an active website and continues to make predictions and write books. He continues to be seen as one of the foremost spokesmen for premillennial dispensationalism, and is certainly among the most popular. His books, even after *The Late Great Planet Earth*, have been bestselling, and he has a loyal internet following on sites such as raptureready.com.

The most distressing consequence of Lindsey's method—if not his own words—is Christian Zionism. Although not exclusively a premillennial dispensationalist movement, Lindsey's book (and others) have popularized Christian Zionism and certainly have seen it as a part of their belief systems. This way of thinking stresses that, before the rapture can occur, Israel must be secured as a homeland for Jewish people and the temple must be rebuilt in Jerusalem. Unfortunately, it has led to a view of Israelis and Palestinians as pawns in a cosmic (Christian) game; Jews must be moved back to Israel to establish a base for the return of Jesus, and Palestinians must be removed from their homes, forcibly and illegally if necessary, to accomplish the same. In the end, of course, Christian Zionists believe the return of Jesus will result in both groups' destruction. Many Christian groups in the United States and abroad have roundly denounced this type of Christian Zionism, since it ultimately calls for a violent end to the humans who live (or wish to live) in Israel.

 DAVID KORESH AND WACO

WHAT WAS IT?

In 1993, the U.S. Bureau of Alcohol, Tobacco and Firearms entered into a stand-off with the Branch Davidians of Mt. Carmel, outside of Waco, Texas. The Branch Davidian group was a small sect which had ties to the Adventist movement. The leader of this group at the time, David Koresh, had been convinced for years that he and his fellow believers were preparing for an apocalyptic battle, based on his reading of the book of Revelation. He saw himself as the messiah in this coming war. The initial stage of the 1993 stand-off, which left several ATF agents and Davidians dead, only intensified Koresh's belief that the end of days was upon them. It is unclear, however, whether the Davidians would have used the weapons and "army" they had been amassing; the stand-off with the ATF and FBI came to a disturbing end when a fire engulfed the compound and killed most of the Davidians inside.

Mount Carmel was an Adventist community and held apocalyptic beliefs long before David Koresh became involved in it. As we have discussed, the Seventh-Day Adventist Church was an outgrowth of the Great Disappointment of the 1830s. After the Disappointment, apocalyptic fervor did not disappear from the SDA; indeed, it remained an important part of their worldview, and millennial expectation informed their theology. The doctrinal statement *Seventh-Day Adventists Believe* notes that the remnant (i.e., faithful SDA membership) will be marked by prophetic gifts and faithfulness to the true Sabbath in the time of tribulation, until Jesus returns in accordance with a literalist reading of the Revelation. Here, we see several important features that will be key for understanding of the Davidians as they developed under Koresh: first, Adventists have long seen themselves as the remnant, the 144,000 true believers who will inherit the kingdom of God after the time of tribulation; second, the Adventists have long asserted that other groups (such as Christians who worship on Sunday) are not faithful to the commands of the Bible as they alone are; third, Adventists believe strongly in the continuation of prophecy and the possibility that God would speak through individuals in the here-and-now. These beliefs were a foundation onto which Koresh built his understanding of the last days.

Victor Houteff founded the sanctuary at Mt. Carmel in 1935 outside of Waco, Texas. He was actually the one to call those who lived there "Davidians," in anticipation of their role

129

in the messianic kingdom to come. As a further eschatological reminder, he apparently set a clock in the main house to 11:00 p.m. to illustrate how little time remained until the end. Houteff's widow also played an important role in promoting the apocalyptic atmosphere of the place. She set the date of the Second Coming for April 22, 1959, convincing many that on that day the true believers would be raised to heaven, so they ought to sell their possessions, come to the compound, and prepare to be raptured. When her prediction did not come to pass, and she died, a split ensued. One side of the split was led by Ben Roden. His group "The Branch" believed that the apocalyptic events Mrs. Houteff predicted had indeed begun and that they were the first harvest of God in the imminent apocalypse who would be under the coming leadership of a seventh angel as described in Revelation 10:7. The leaders that followed over the next thirty-four years continued the apocalyptic fervor exhibited by the group's founders until the arrival of David Koresh.

David Koresh (born Vernon Howell) was raised in the SDA tradition and attended an SDA school, and, later, a church in Tyler, Texas. However, after claiming to receive several visions (including one about marrying the pastor's daughter), he was disfellowshipped from that congregation and subsequently came into contact with the community at Mt. Carmel in 1981. At Mt. Carmel, his visions were recognized as prophetic; his status was further confirmed by a trip to Israel, during which he claimed he was given the key to understanding the seven seals discussed in the Revelation, and the knowledge that he was the seventh angel hoped for by the Branch Davidians. Within a decade (and not without some major power struggles), Koresh became the sole leader of Mt. Carmel. Within one year, the community was clearly marked by his theological principles, most notably the New Light Doctrine.

As with most aspects of the group, the New Light Doctrine was related to Koresh's apocalyptic understandings. By this point, Koresh had asserted that, in his dual roles as the seventh angel and anointed prophet, he had also become the messianic figure ("Christ spirit") who would rule over the new creation when the tribulation ended. (Koresh believed that humanity was currently experiencing the tribulation, or time of trials and suffering that preceded the new creation.) Koresh and his followers further believed that, as the messianic king, Koresh bore the sole responsibility to populate the post-apocalyptic kingdom. Thus, in the New Light Doctrine, Koresh asserted that he was commanded by God to be the only one in the community to have intercourse with the female members, and that no other man was allowed to engage in sexual activity of any sort. Between 1989 and 1993, Koresh had sex with fifteen members of the community, some as young as thirteen (Newport 199, 201). By the time of the raid, most of the children in the compound at Mt. Carmel had been fathered by Koresh.

It appears that the members of the compound became increasingly expectant of the eschaton during the Koresh era. In the 1980s Koresh had predicted that the end would be upon the believers in 1995; however, governmental investigations of the sect seem to have pushed up the timeline (Thompson 295). The

Branch Davidians (along with the SDA more generally) had long held that one clear sign of the end was the arrival of the two beasts from Revelation 13; the first was identified early on as the non-SDA church (particularly the Catholic Church), and the second was expected to be the United States, at the time when it became belligerent toward the Adventists (Newport 235). In the Branch Davidian compound at Mt. Carmel, the uptick in investigations by U.S. government groups, such as the visits of child safety investigators in 1992, seemed to signal that the time was at hand (Thompson 295). In this same period, Koresh and the Branch members increased their purchase of weapons and weapon-making materials, which came to the attention of the Bureau of Alcohol, Tobacco and Firearms, the ATF.

The raid on Mt. Carmel on February 28, 1993—and the final assault that resulted in the fire on April 18—has been much debated (Wessinger 57). Since this book deals with apocalyptic movements, we will not focus on who bears responsibility for the tragedy. Instead, the focus here is on the way the Davidians perceived the siege and the role of biblical interpretation and eschatological expectation in that perception.

Koresh and the Davidians believed the Psalms predicted the end times, but as we have seen, the book of Psalms is not apocalyptic material. However, because they were "of David," Koresh believed they would describe the Davidic kingdom and the role of Koresh (the new David) in the coming kingdom. Psalm 2 was perhaps the most important apocalyptic prophecy for the Davidians; in it, "The kings of the earth set themselves, and the rulers take counsel together, against the Lord and his anointed" (vv. 2–3). Especially after the initial raid, Koresh believed himself to be confirmed as the Lord's anointed, his Christ; the "kings of the earth" referred to the U.S. government and its agents. He saw the time of the siege as time to get out the message of the government's betrayal of the Branch and the faithful, and to send a warning that this meant the time of the end was near. Indeed, he was so convinced that Psalm 2 was being fulfilled in the siege that he wrote an "Exposition of the Seven Seals" during this time to demonstrate how near he believed the end to be.

The seven seals, of course, refer to events in the Revelation that signal the end. In a radio interview, and in discussions with FBI negotiators, it seems clear that Koresh saw the raid as the opening of the fifth seal discussed in Revelation:

> [John] saw under the altar the souls of those who had been slaughtered for the word of God and for the testimony they had given; they cried out with a loud voice, "Sovereign Lord, holy and true, how long will it be before you judge and avenge our blood on the inhabitants of the earth?" They were each given a white robe and told to rest a little longer, until the number would be complete both of their fellow servants and of their brothers and sisters, who were soon to be killed as they themselves had been killed. (Rev. 6:9–11)

In the initial raid, five Davidians were killed by gunfire, and this seemed confirmation that the fifth seal was opened and that the siege was a brief period of waiting, in which the dead would "rest a little longer." Koresh further interpreted these words to mean that the rest of the members of the community were about to be killed, only to be raised again to fight the final apocalyptic battle, a process they called "translation." When the Branch Davidians originally agreed to end the siege by surrender on March 2, several believed that they would "translate" as they exited the compound. However, Koresh pulled back from the decision to surrender, and the martyrdom of the remaining members was delayed. The final fire on April 19 took the lives of seventy-four members of the community and certainly must have appeared to those on the inside—whether they wished to die or not—to be the final confirmation that the fifth seal was indeed opened.

WHAT WERE THE CONSEQUENCES OF THE FAILURE?

Of course, the most significant and tragic consequence of the events of February—April 1993 was the profound loss of life. Four ATF agents were killed in the initial raid, and a total of eighty Davidians were killed in that event and in the final fire. But it is unclear if these consequences were the direct result of the apocalyptic beliefs of the Branch members or if the actions of the ATF and FBI simply confirmed for them something that they had seen coming but never intended to instigate. Strong arguments have been made on both sides and again, that is beyond the scope of this discussion. What is clear is that the apocalyptic beliefs of the Davidians colored their every thought and action during that period.

This discussion barely scratches the surface of the complicated biblical interpretation behind the beliefs of the Branch Davidians at Mt. Carmel. However, it does help us see that, while the Davidians may have been labeled as a cult full of crazies out to get the government, in actuality they bore a striking resemblance to apocalyptic movements throughout history. Consider that, like nearly every other group we've discussed, (1) the community saw themselves as possessing true knowledge and proper religious practice; (2) the community believed they were persecuted by individual and political forces for those beliefs and practices; and (3) the community reinterpreted sacred texts to make sense of their persecution and to offer comfort and hope to the members. In this, the Davidians at Mt. Carmel were no different from the Shakers, or the Anabaptists, or the participants of the Bar Kochba revolt. Indeed, in this they were much like the communities that produced apocalyptic literature in the first place. This is not an attempt to excuse any improper acts that were committed by Koresh or others, but simply to suggest that—when it comes to apocalypticism—Patmos and Waco might not be terribly far apart.

The Waco tragedy should also convict us to seek understanding and conversation with potentially violent apocalyptic sects rather than quickly resorting to military action. Perhaps if the government negotiators had instigated negotiation before the initial raid, Koresh might not have believed the fifth seal had been opened at all. Negotiation before the assault might have prevented the tragedy entirely.

SPACESHIP APOCALYPSES

WHAT WERE THEY?

In the late 1990s, three different apocalyptic sects predicted that the end of this world would be accompanied by the arrival of an alien spaceship. All three, the Planetary Activation Organization, the Heaven's Gate community, and the True Way were most active in the United States, although the third originated in Taiwan. Further, all three shared a worldview that combined elements of Christian apocalypticism with other religious or para-religious beliefs.

The Planetary Activation Organization was founded by New York native Sheldan Nidle, who claimed to be a psychic. The PAO claims that Nidle's experiences with extraterrestrial life began early in his life:

> [Nidle's] experiences began shortly after his birth and were highlighted all through his childhood by various modes of contact phenomena, as well as accompanying manifestation—light-form communications, extraterrestrial visitations, and teaching/learning sessions on board spacecraft. During most of his life, he has enjoyed ongoing telepathic communications and direct "core knowledge" inserts (etheric and physical implants). (See http://www.paoweb.com/bio .htm)

Since the time of those first apparent contacts, Nidle claims to have received messages that the end of the current age of humanity is imminent. Nidle believes that when the time is right, and at the direction of a Supreme Being, beings from the

Galactic Federation will make contact with the inhabitants of earth and usher in a new era of human consciousness in which our minds are not narrowed by earthly limitations. From this point a new world government will be instituted, the "Spiritual Hierarchy," to direct the planet until it encounters a photon belt of energy that will usher in an era of paradisiacal consciousness for all of creation.

In the meantime, Nidle believes, humanity must strive to be worthy of the coming first contact, employing a process called ascension to improve themselves by emulating the Ascended Masters of Light, including Jesus. If one is able to reach the full consciousness modeled by these masters, one becomes a Galactic Human. The Galactic Humans work with Ascended Masters and angels to prepare humanity for the world to come. (A splinter group within the movement calls these people "The Ground Crew.") While full consciousness is a goal for all of humanity, not all humans are poised to ascend; some are more likely to possess the disposition and longing that causes them to question their limited human experience. These people are called "starseeds." According to the PAO website, starseeds are described in the following way:

> [They] experience the aloneness and separateness that is the human condition, but also have the sense of being foreigners on this planet. They find the behavior and motives of our society puzzling and illogical. Starseeds are often most reluctant to become involved in the institutions of society, e.g. political, economic, health care, etc. Even at an early age, they tend to discern the hidden agendas of such conventions

with unusual clarity. (See http://www.paoweb.com/starseed
.htm)

In fact, according to Nidle, starseeds are not of this planet. They are instead beings from other planets who are reborn here, in an amnesiac state, only to be "activated" at a predetermined moment. When they are, the limits of their consciousness will be lifted, and they will be able to fulfill their mission to assist in bringing about the earth's Golden Age.

Nidle first predicted the advent of extraterrestrials in 1996, believing they would arrive by December of 1997, but he has removed all these predictions from his website. Professor Andreas Grünschloß has written an article on the group containing information on these failed prophecies. (See http://wwwuser.gwdg.de/~agruens/UFO/ufocargo_final.html #FNT28)

When the ships (supposedly about 16 million of them, arriving with a fleet of angels) did not appear, Nidle inevitably cast his predictions into the near future. He has since latched on to a date at the end of 2012, saying on his website:

> Another change is that the yearly time-line is also accelerating. Many persons who study time have noticed that recently, years have been reduced seemingly to months. In this regard, many psychics who have encountered the year 2012 AD have noticed that it contains a block around the magical date of December 21, 2012. This date is the one picked by the Mayan calendar as the end of time on this planet as we now know it! These coincidences point to the fact that this period is one in which our planet is

moving towards a new reality. (See http://www.paoweb.com/ firstime.htm)

Nidle is still actively updating his webpage.

While Nidle's view of the apocalypse assumes that aliens will come to us and bring a heavenly age on earth, the members of the Heaven's Gate community believed that followers needed to leave the earth behind to board the alien ship that was coming to meet them behind the Hale-Bopp comet in 1997. In the 1970s the group that eventually became known as Heaven's Gate was founded by Marshall Applewhite and Bonnie Lu Nettles, who called themselves "The Two." The couple claimed they received a revelation that they (collectively) were Jesus Christ reincarnated; the reincarnation had been made possible with the assistance of extraterrestrial life and made them representatives of the Next Level. They moved to California from the Midwest and began to preach their gospel to the disenfranchised there. Over the next twenty years, the movement both gathered and lost many followers with everything culminating in a mass suicide in 1997. Some of the members that eventually participated in the mass suicide were the earliest converts to the movement, and some were recent converts.

The beliefs of the Heaven's Gate religious movement evolved and changed over time, but the basic beliefs can be summarized. For believers, the human body is merely a vehicle that nurtures a soul, which is implanted into the faithful from the Next Level (or The Level Above Human, or The Kingdom of Heaven). Not all humans have a soul. Those who don't are known as mammalian humans, little more than animals that walk upright. The soul of true humans, as in Hindu and Buddhist philosophies of reincarnation, passes through various "vehicles" over time and is reimplanted into new bodies each time. Those who have been implanted with a soul ought to nurture that soul through close (but nonsexual) contact with a representative from the Next Level such as Applewhite, in a process known as grafting, to purify and protect that gift. Catherine Wessinger described grafting this way:

> By being devoted to serving their Representative, their Older Member, who was their sole means of entering the Kingdom of Heaven, the disciples aimed to become instruments of the mind of their Older Member. In this manner, they cultivated the advanced thinking and consciousness of The Level Above Human (236).

Grafting involved leaving family, friends, employment, physical pleasures, and all desires behind. By so doing, the disciple could protect her or his mind from evil aliens (Luciferians) who wished to inhibit the growth of the soul. If one could overcome all desires, it was possible to end the cycle of rebirth and enter The Level Above Human.

Heaven's Gate was, like the Planetary Activation Organization, a mix of Christian apocalyptic theology and other religious beliefs. From Christianity, Nettles and Applewhite drew language that the end of the world was fast approaching. At one point they claimed that they would be martyred and resurrected in accordance with their reading of Revelation 11:3–11. Applewhite also claimed to be the second coming of Christ, and the group used grafting and harvest imagery to describe the apocalypse in a similar way to how those images appear in Johannine literature (the books of John, 1–3 John, and Revelation). The Two also drew on Christian imagery for the forces opposed to their movement. The Two called their mistreatment by the press "assassination," which fulfilled their so-called prediction that they would be martyred and resurrected (Wessinger 234). The evil space aliens were called Luciferians or collectively known as the Antichrist, borrowing language from 1, 2, and 3 John. Applewhite complemented these Christian allusions with theology borrowed from Theosophy, Hinduism, Buddhism, and New Age movements.

A THIRD APOCALYPTIC UFO GROUP, THE TRUE WAY, PREDICTED THE ARRIVAL OF DOOMSDAY JUST ONE YEAR AFTER THE HEAVEN'S GATE SUICIDES.

The Heaven's Gate group, prior to the decision to take their own lives, repeatedly and publically announced that the earth was in a state beyond repair, that it was about to be recycled, and that only those who had accepted the teaching of Applewhite and Nettles would be spirited away from the cataclysm. Throughout the late seventies and eighties, The Two taught that this rapture would happen by means of a spaceship. Even after Nettles' death from cancer, Applewhite continued to predict the arrival of a flying saucer into the early nineties. In one of the most famous episodes, disciples (then known as the Total Overcomers) gathered at the Santa Monica Pier in 1994 in expectation of a ship's arrival, once again to be disappointed. (See http://www.laweekly.com/2007-03-22/news/they-walk-among-us/)

Applewhite began to question if perhaps it was necessary to leave behind the earthly vehicle to achieve reunification with the Next Level. By 1997, Applewhite and the remaining members of Heaven's Gate felt the time had come: the Hale-Bopp comet was approaching, and they believed that hidden behind it was the long-awaited ship. In March 1997, over three days, thirty-nine members of the group, including Applewhite, took a mix of phenobarbitals in applesauce and vodka, covered their heads in plastic bags, and died, a process called "membership in the Next Level." A surviving group member found the members (ages 26–72), lying on individual bunks wearing identical outfits (black shirts, sweatpants, black and white Nikes, and armbands) and covered in purple shrouds, at the community compound in Rancho Santa Fe, California.

A third apocalyptic UFO group, the True Way (also known as God's Salvation Church, Chen Tao, and the God Saves the Earth Flying Saucer Foundation), predicted the arrival of doomsday just one year after the Heaven's Gate suicides. Given the horror of the mass suicide in California, it is understandable that the residents of Garland, Texas were a bit disconcerted by the arrival of one hundred fifty True Way transplants from Taiwan, who descended on that city in 1997. Their founder and leader, Hon-Ming Chen, settled the families in Garland because the name sounded like "God's Land" and resonated with Pure Land Buddhist ideals of a Western Paradise protected from evil.

The residents of Garland found, however, that their new neighbors were not a secretive group, nor were they interested in mass suicide should the end not arrive as predicted. Individual religious studies scholars, Taiwanese officials in Houston, and the Garland Police Department confirmed that the group was unlikely to threaten themselves or anyone else (Kliever 45). Chen repeatedly denounced suicide and made clear that the group members were free to come and go as they wished.

After the Chen Tao families arrived in autumn of 1997, Teacher Chen held a news conference in which he revealed that God would appear on television (worldwide on channel 18) on March 25, 1998. This appearance would be a preview of God's arrival in Chen's front yard one week later. At that time, God would shake the hand of anyone present, speak to the person in his or her own language, and prepare for the apocalypse by organizing the evacuation of earth from Gary, Indiana, on spaceships. According to the *Times* of London, Chen's front yard contained a sign that read, "God is going to change into man to meet the people of the world at this house on March 31, 1998. Everyone is welcome to witness God's descending at 10 a.m. that day." (March 15, 1998).

Chen's preaching, as we have seen with Heaven's Gate and the PAO, combined elements of Christian apocalypticism and other religions. God's offer of spaceships to the faithful allowed them to avoid what believers called the Great Tribulation of 1999, in which nuclear war would break out and destroy the earth. The term *Great Tribulation* is reminiscent of language in Daniel, Mark, and 1 Thessalonians. Chen further revealed that he believed that he had fathered Jesus Christ two thousand years prior and that one of the children in his community was a reincarnation or second coming of Jesus. He showed photos of jet trails that contained the number 007 as proof that UFOs were preparing for the coming end (Shlachter, *Fort Worth Star-Telegram*), drawing on the common numerological tradition in apocalyptic texts. Along with these Christian allusions, Chen also drew from Eastern religions, particularly the Pure Land Buddhist idea of a Western paradise, which he interpreted literally to mean the Western Hemisphere (particularly Texas).

Pure Land Buddhism is a sect of Buddhism which believes that human beings can help their own chances of attaining Nirvana by requesting the help of a divine figure named Amitabha. By calling on his name, the believer is reborn into a Western paradise. In this paradise, it is much easier for a believer to follow the moral commands of the religion and attain Nirvana.

God did not appear on television on March 25, and Chen met with the press to inform them that God had made another plan and that while the media could consider his date for the arrival of God on the lawn "nonsense," the believers would "keep on anticipating the date of God's coming on the 31st" (quoted. in Kliever 50). One week later, Chen spoke to the press again, reinterpreting the prophetic message of God's arrival. The address has been summarized this way:

God has arrived in my [Chen's] front yard as predicted because each of you are God. If you join your right and left hands, you have shaken hands with God as predicted. And each of you can understand God in your own thoughts and in your own language. (Kliever 50)

By the end of May, most of the members of the church had left Texas, but a small group followed the teacher to Lockport, New York. There, Chen suggested, souls would gather "and receive the super high-tech training from God for piloting airplanes and flying saucers" (*Ottawa Citizen* 2000). However, when this prophecy also failed to materialize, the group fell apart completely, and has not been active since 2001.

WHAT WERE THE CONSEQUENCES OF THE FAILURE?

The fallout of the failed predictions was quite different in each case. There is a compelling case that can be made for the differences in structure and demands on the community as at least one determining factor in the outcome. In her work on violent millennial groups, Catherine Wessinger notes that certain features in religious movements point to potential catastrophe, while others are reassuring. Among the "red flags" for potential violence, she includes:

💣 being persecuted

💣 social alienation

💣 resistance to investigation

💣 withdrawal to an isolated location

- dependence on a charismatic leader
- loss of personal identity, associations, and livelihood if members leave
- access to information about the outside world is controlled by the leader (276–280)

However, she notes there is much less reason for concern in cases where the group does or feels the following:

- no sense of being attacked by opponents
- the group openly answers questions about its beliefs and practices
- the group recruits new members to offer them salvation (281)

The characteristics that Wessinger describes fits the three UFO-focused apocalyptic movements to different degrees.

The PAO remains quite active on the Internet, and Nidle continues to predict the arrival of the spacecraft very soon. On their site, the PAO recommends that in preparation believers should organize themselves into Planetary Activation Groups, meeting either in person or on the internet (NetPAGs). The group meetings include:

- Being current with Sheldan Nidle's bi-weekly updates
- Discussing the updates
- Meditating together

♦ Doing rituals initiated by them or requested by the Spiritual Hierarchy of the Earth

♦ Practicing Fluid Management

♦ Inventorying members' expertise and talents

♦ Setting up goals for their group

♦ Allowing members to solve problems as a group, using individual expertise

♦ Helping individuals within the group to go through their healing process

♦ Connecting with other groups to exchange information and mutual experiences

♦ Helping to activate people outside the PAG group through contact or networking[7][[missing endnote info]]

All of these suggested activities are rather low-intensity and low-commitment, as far as religious groups go, and we can see that many of Wessinger's "reassuring characteristics" are present. While the role of the movement's leader is important, the community also plays a role in forming its own understanding of the faith (as with building their own rituals and setting their own goals). The result is that the religion is de-centered and not reliant on the authority figure to give all direction and meaning to the community. Further, the group is not isolated but encouraged to "activate" others and connect with other groups. Finally, the movement maintains a sense of optimism and lacks the paranoia or feelings of persecution that characterize some more violent apocalyptic groups.

Similarly, Chen Tao, while having more red flag features such as centralized leadership, remained open with the media, resisted violence, and allowed free movement to its disciples. When the end failed to arrive, most simply left the group and returned to Taiwan. There were no consequences to their exit, as there are in the most high-intensity religious groups.

In the case of Heaven's Gate, however, many of the most troubling features were present. The group saw themselves as not of this planet nor at home in their own bodies (social alienation); they lived isolated, and moved often, even before renting the communal house in Rancho Santa Fe; Applewhite served as a strong charismatic leader, insisted on group discipline, and was the authority on group matters; the group members, and especially its leaders, felt themselves persecuted by the world. The mass suicide at Heaven's Gate was the largest to take place on American soil, and it was a tragic end to a very long process of isolation and despairing as the end failed to arrive time after time.

YEAR 2000-RELATED APOCALYPSES

WHAT WERE THEY?

We have repeatedly seen that the idea of the "millennium," the thousand-year reign of Christ described in Revelation 20, is important to many apocalyptic groups' mindsets. We looked at how some believed strongly that the 1000-year reign of Christ would be completed in the year 1000. And as we have also seen, by the time of the dispensationalist movement of the late twentieth century, disagreements about the meaning and timing of the millennial reign were heated because Christians were divided into amillennialist, premillennialist, and postmillennialist camps. The arrival of the year 2000 did nothing to ease these disputes. In fact the addition of the possibility of a technological Armageddon in the form of the "Y2K bug" caused many literalist Christian interpreters to fear the worst.

Originally the fear of the Y2K bug had very little to do with religious belief. The "bug" was a highly publicized problem with the way early computer systems had been programmed to store dates. In most computer systems, the months, days, and years were stored as two digits apiece; computer memory at the time was expensive, and using only two digits saved memory. So, for example, a credit card that expired in September of 1999 was stored as 0999—the ninth month in 1999. Later, as computer memory became cheaper and more plentiful, the old software was not changed for fear of introducing inadvertent errors into the code. However, as the year 2000 approached, programmers realized that after the year 2000 dates would be calculated incorrectly, thus creating problems for any industry that makes use of the date, like banking and finance, manufacturing, and security. Millions of dollars were spent in the U.S. alone to correct this programming problem by reprogramming software to use a four-digit year code. The programmers who made the coding adjustments expressed more concern about the growing public hysteria than any of the potential glitches (Newman 276).

The Y2K bug itself, then, was not an insurmountable technical obstacle, but the portrayal of the issue in the press was often over-hyped. The media emphasized the most drastic potential consequences, including a complete failure of the American electronic economy, looting, martial law, and societal collapse. In a discussion of how the media portrayal of the problem contributed to fears that the economy would fail and looting and chaos would ensue, Gregg Hoffman wrote:

> [The media] establish[ed] "experts," not unlike priests and philosophers, to decipher the language for us and engender faith in them as conveyers of truth. In a few cases, these "experts" resemble[d] the leaders of various religious groups that periodically predict the end of the world. (98)

Given the complex, technological nature of the Y2K bug, it is no surprise that the public put their trust in the pronouncements of media "experts" and their predictions, even if they lacked the programming knowledge to assure the public that it was possible to resolve this problem in time.

Once Y2K began to get media attention, subsequent news stories focused on those people who, fearing the worst, were setting up bunkers, hoarding food, or stockpiling weapons for fear of an extended period of calamity. Soon, at least in popular imagination, Y2K became synonymous with apocalyptic devastation.

Christian media in the United States was not exempt from the hysteria surrounding the Y2K bug. Members of the Christian press took the secular, technological concerns and combined those with their religious visions of the apocalypse and millennium; they then promoted that interpretation (Cowan). Andrea Tapia, a professor of information sciences and technology, confirmed this finding in her study as well, noting, "[Information about Y2K] was more often than not [from] a media source. . . . Over half of the subjects listened to Christian radio shows and watched Christian television" (273). Tapia even noted that most of her respondents relied on one radio personality, Chuck Missler, and that his concern fueled their fear of the apocalypse (ibid.). When combined, the fears of the economic collapse in America and the millennialist concerns of some conservative Christians resulted in a rise in apocalyptic enthusiasm and preaching. Many others took advantage of the growing millennialist fervor; according to McMinn, *Christianity Today* sold ads for Y2K related "survival products" beginning early in 1999 (207).

While not all those who warned of impending disaster offered predictions as to the exact nature of the catastrophe, some believed that the feared electronic banking problems would give rise to a cashless society, a forerunner of the apocalypse in their minds. The fear of a cashless society was related to their interpretation of the "mark of the beast" imagery in Revelation, since without it "no one can buy or sell" (Rev. 13:17). Tapia notes that one Christian writer believed the computer at the World Bank itself to be the Antichrist (269).

When January 1, 2000, arrived, a few technical problems were reported, but nothing on the scale offered by media "experts" and Christian writers. The U.S. Government's report, entitled *Y2K Aftermath—Crisis Averted*, listed several minor issues reported domestically, including "Medicare payment delays, double billing by some credit card companies, degradation of a spy satellite system, [and] 911 problems in several localities" (9). They also noted that, internationally, the Hong Kong Futures Exchange had what they termed an "outage," along with a few other minor issues they could report. However, overall, the report concluded that "no major problems were experienced in the U.S. or worldwide during the millennium date change" (10).

Aside from the fears of technological Armageddon, some apocalyptic thinkers based their predictions of the end solely on the basis of the turning of the calendar. Hal Lindsey famously predicted Armageddon to take place in 2000 (after it did not happen in the 1980s, as he had earlier predicted). Michael Drosnin, author of *The Bible Code*, also foresaw the end occurring in that year based on information he found "hidden" in the Torah. Many of these predictions were mere curiosities, and passed along with the changing of the date, but on occasion the failure of these prophecies to materialize led to disastrous consequences.

Two Ugandans, Joseph Kibwetere and Keredonia Mwerinde, founded the Movement for the Restoration of the Ten Commandments of God (MRTCG) in approximately 1989. Both Kibwetere and Mwerinde reported having visions of the Virgin Mary and Jesus, and the group drew their rules and apocalyptic prophecies from these visions. By the time of the production of their published work, *A Timely Message from Heaven: The End of the Present Times*, in 1996, it appears that the group believed that the apocalypse would arrive soon to punish the Catholic

Church, from whom they were disenfranchised, as well as the corrupt nations of the world for failing to live up to the standard of the Ten Commandments. The MRTCG set a year 2000 deadline for the apocalypse, announcing that the world would not see 2001 (Mayer 207).

The MRTCG claimed that Uganda was the "New Israel" that would be spared. The other nations would face biblical plagues and other forms of destruction; the Russians, for example, would experience destruction by locusts, and Mozambique by "its own machinery." In his investigation of their handbook, Dean Murphy notes:

> [T]he cult's handbook speaks of three days of darkness, during which "those who had repented" will gather in safe houses known as arks. About a quarter of the world's population will survive the Earth's cleansing, with the rest being thrown into hell. The new world, according to the prophecy, will be flat like a pancake and will be connected to heaven. Death will be vanquished, and Satan and his followers "put in fetters." (*Los Angeles Times* "153 More Bodies Tied to Ugandan Cult Unearthed," March 2000)

The language here is clearly reminiscent of Revelation, particularly in the vanquishing of death and Satan, but also draws heavily on the Noah traditions of the Hebrew Bible and 1 Enoch, especially in its employment of "ark" imagery for the safe houses in the coming destruction and renewal of the earth.

In preparation for this cleansing of the earth, the faithful were commanded to live a disciplined collective existence, without alcohol, sexual activity, or verbal communication (which could lead to false witness, contrary to the Commandments). Believers were expected to fast and pray regularly, and allowed to sleep very little (Walliss 54).

Reports differ on the events immediately preceding the fire, but apparently many of the adherents of the Movement sold all their possessions and left their families in the hopes of receiving a painless life post-apocalypse. It seems that the leaders were emphasizing a March 17, 2000, date for the rapture of the faithful from the holy place of Kanungu. After that, it would be only a short time of tribulation until the new earth was formed:

> [The new earth] would be like "Heaven on Earth" . . . for those who would have gathered in Kanungu. There would be constant visitation of people coming from Heaven to Earth. All the needs of the followers would be cared for. There would be a New Earth, on which no work would have to be done anymore. (Mayer 207).

In religious historian Jean-Francois Mayer's field notes on the Movement, he acknowledges the appeal of such an apocalypse to those who had survived war, extreme poverty, and devastating disease. However, it seems that by March 17 of that year, when the anticipated end did not arrive, there was dissention within the group and dissatisfaction amongst members with the continual delay and reinterpretation of the rapture (Walliss 62).

It appears that this internal pressure led group leaders to systematically murder dissenters in the few months leading up to the fire in March. Discoveries of mass graves in the area support this theory, as the deceased were clearly victims of violence and a cover-up (Walliss 50). The leaders of the sect systematically murdered nearly a thousand members. On March 17, 2000, more than five hundred members of the sect were in the MRTCG church with the windows and doors nailed shut. An initial explosion and subsequent fire destroyed the building, killing all of the individuals inside. While immediately after the fire the media described the event as collective suicide, it now appears that the MRTCG leadership orchestrated the event and that those inside the church were unaware that they were about to perish.

WHAT WERE THE CONSEQUENCES OF THE FAILURE?

It is intriguing, if also quite sad, to note the two very different consequences from these two sets of year 2000 predictions. When dawn broke on January 1, with only a few Y2K bug glitches and nothing serious to report, the crisis was averted (to borrow the U.S. Government's phrase), and things went on as before. Cowan has noted that those who predicted the apocalypse in association with Y2K responded to the "failed failure" by revisionism, defiance, or reinterpretation and conspiracy theories, but with generally harmless results (76–79).

However, the same prophetic failure had disastrous consequences in Uganda. This most likely is the result of the intense commitment of the MRTCG. The profound difference in access to wealth and power also likely played a huge role. As we have seen so many times, the most passionate apocalyptic hopes are often from among the most socially and economically disadvantaged. In this case, for the people of Uganda—struggling as they were against poverty, violence, and disease—the draw of freedom from those fears must have been quite powerful. Those who did join the Movement invested still more in the apocalypse by their commitment to strict discipline and by the abandonment of their possessions and families. When the end did not arrive, it is no surprise that dissatisfaction and dissent was impossible to ignore. That is not to say that the members of the Movement might not have left peacefully were it not for the actions of their leadership, only that the intensity of the response would have been unlikely to occur in the less economically challenged and less strictly disciplined groups who faced the Y2K challenge in the U.S.

Like the year 1000, the year 2000 is just another number. Yes, references are rife in ancient materials to millennia as markers of apocalyptic time, but there is nothing to indicate—even in the most conservative readings of the biblical text—that there is something particularly significant about a date like 2000 CE. After all, the calendar on which that number is based is likely off by at least four years, given our best archaeological and textual evidence for the birth of Jesus. Even if one suggested the millennial reign of Christ were literal, then perhaps 1000, or 1030, would be a candidate for apocalyptic obsession, but not 2000. Further, since there is no "year zero" in the common calendar, even if all other things were accurate, the new millennium didn't really dawn until January 2001. (See N. T. Wright's "Apocalypse Now?" for a discussion of the futility of dating the apocalypse based on a millennial emphasis.)

HAROLD CAMPING AND FAMILY RADIO

WHAT WAS IT?

Harold Camping is the founder of (and was, until recently, a radio host at) Family Radio, a conservative Christian radio station that stoked the apocalyptic fever of thousands with predictions of the end of the world in 1994 and again in May of 2011 (along with a companion prediction for the completion of the end in October of the same year). His station raised millions to get word of the end on billboards, pamphlets, and the radio. In response to Camping's prophecy of the end, which relied heavily on calculations using "significant" biblical numbers, many people throughout the world preached on the streets, took out ads in their local newspapers, sold their possessions, and in some cases committed acts of violence.

Harold Camping, now 90 years old, was raised in California, and it was there he first became interested in using radio to promote his reading of the Bible. Together with two others, Camping purchased a station in San Francisco, California, in 1958. Five years later, Camping began broadcasting his signature live call-in show, *Open Forum*. On this show, Camping promoted his understanding of complete biblical inerrancy, in which every word in the Bible was accurate, factual, scientific, and—above all—predictive of coming events. It was on *Open Forum*, in 1992, that Camping announced that his biblical study had yielded the exact date of the rapture (that is, the physical raising of "saved" humans from the earth at the beginning of the apocalypse): September 6, 1994. And, it was by means of this same program, nearly two decades later, that he spread his corrected date for the rapture. He continued broadcasting the show until he suffered a stroke in 2011.

Camping's method of proving the date of the rapture relies heavily on numbers and calculation. To arrive at the May 21, 2011, date, Camping took "significant" numbers from the biblical text (7, 12, 23, etc.) and clues he discovered in the text (such as Jesus' vision of the destroyed temple in Matt. 24) and used them to draw conclusions about certain key historical moments (such as the "end of the church age"). From there, he expanded the timetable forward, again using significant numbers, to count out the tribulation period, the rapture, and the end. For example, consider Camping's discussion of how long the tribulation period would last:

> [T]he period of great tribulation is definitely a time when God is preparing the churches and the world for God's wrath, which will immediately follow this period. The numbers 7 and 23 both became increasingly relevant when we discovered that precisely 8,400 days equal a full 23 years. The number 8,400 equals 7x12x100, thus allowing the number 7 and the number 23 to be featured by an 8,400, that is, 23-year, great tribulation period. (*We Are Almost There!* 46)

Camping believed strongly that God was acting in knowable, orderly ways, as this quotation makes clear. The significant numbers, 7 and 23 here, would have to play a role—in his words, "be featured"—because for Camping, God's faithfulness was numerically precise. In an article in *New York Magazine*,

Camping displayed a similar approach to predicting the date of the rapture as May 21:

> "The atonement or redemption demonstrated by Christ's suffering and death on April 1, 33 AD (the number 5) is 100% completed on May 21, 2011 (the number 10) when all the true believers are raptured into Heaven (the number 17)," he explained. Multiplying those numbers, and squaring them to show His emphasis, gives you 722,500, an "enormously significant" sum equal to the exact number of days between the two dates [of the crucifixion and the end of the world]. (Lee)

The May 21 date would be marked, Camping believed, by massive earthquakes at 6 p.m. local time around the world; then the elect would be taken to heaven to be spared the wrath of God which was to follow. A five-month period of devastation would greet those not raptured, and the complete destruction of the world would occur on October 21 of that same year.

Camping was so convinced by these calculations that he began a media blitz on his radio program and via billboards, print ads, and pamphlets. *The Los Angeles Times* estimated that worldwide more than $100 million was spent by Family Radio on promotion of the date. In addition to the expenditures of the station, individuals who believed Camping's prediction invested their own money, sometimes their entire savings, on spreading the word. Others quit work to travel in RV caravans with biblical texts and the May 21 date displayed on the side. The story was picked up by both the print and electronic secular and Christian media.

Saturday, May 21, 2011, passed without incident: no earthquakes, no fires, no Judgment, and no sign of the rapture of the elect. Camping spent that weekend in his home and returned to *Open Forum* the following Monday. On the show and in an interview with reporters, he addressed the concerns of the faithful and the questions of the skeptics. The judgment of May 21 was a "spiritual judgment," he said, and God had led him to believe it would be physical so that Camping would not be slack in his preaching. However, the October 21 deadline stood firm, and the physical rapture of believers would still occur at that time.

THE HARM DONE TO FOLLOWERS BY CAMPING'S FAILED PREDICTIONS WAS NOT LIMITED TO THEOLOGICAL. THE HARM WAS ALSO FINANCIAL.

Before the October 21 date, Camping suffered a stroke. His show went on hiatus, and after being released from the hospital he began rehabilitation at his home in Alameda. He continued to assert the October 21 date, but when it passed, he did not speak to reporters again.

WHAT WERE THE CONSEQUENCES OF THE FAILURE?

In March of 2012, Family Radio posted to its website a statement, issued by Camping, in which he apologized for his predictions. It read in part:

> We humbly acknowledge we were wrong about the timing. . . . We must also openly acknowledge that we have no

new evidence pointing to another date for the end of the world. Though many dates are circulating, Family Radio has no interest in even considering another date. . . . [The May 21 prediction was an] incorrect and sinful statement.

Camping's apology has effectively closed this issue for Family Radio. The station still posts messages from him, but his *Open Forum* program is no longer on the air.

In an article for *Religion Dispatches*, Tom Bartlett followed up on the human fallout of Camping's failed predictions. For many of the people he interviewed, the most critical consequence was theological: because they had so pinned their beliefs to this date, the failure of Camping's apocalypse left them lost, with little trust in God, and—like the Millerites—disappointed and adrift. But, Bartlett notes, the harm did not stop there. There was financial ruin, as in the case of the man who had spent his retirement savings to buy an RV for the caravan; there were severed family ties, lost jobs, and fears of insanity. (See www .religiondispatches.org/archive/atheologies/5983/a_year_after _the_non-apocalypse%3A_where_are_they_now/)

The May 21 prediction relied heavily on a proof-texting model of reading the Bible. In *We Are Almost There!* Camping drew on passages of Scripture, piecing them together without critical thought. Words could, in his understanding, be chosen from one biblical book and placed next to another without any sense that this might violate original meaning or intent.

Further, Camping insisted that the Bible offered proofs of the end, and what he really meant was proofs in the mathematical sense. However, to come up with his predictions required mathematical gymnastics on an unprecedented scale. It begs the question, why exactly did the Bible need us to square the product of five, ten, and seventeen "to show [Christ's] emphasis" as Camping asserted? Why not divide by three or increase it by a factor of ten? His decisions seem designed to prove a pre-determined conclusion rather than to honestly search the Scripture. I would certainly agree, as we saw in our discussion of the apocalyptic genre, numbers are significant to revelatory texts. However, numbers are intended to represent concepts; these numbers are not meant to be plugged into a formula.

Finally, Camping's determination that the world would be entirely destroyed on October 21 is shockingly inconsistent with the scriptural message of a new heaven and a new earth. The biblical texts that Camping so strongly believed in do not predict a complete destruction of the world, as Camping so fervently did in those few months in 2011; in biblical texts the earth is always the site and beneficiary of the renewing work of God. Certainly, such a harsh view of the end could motivate some believers, but only by fear and not by love.

It is quite likely that Camping believed he was right in his predictions up until the moment of failure; clearly, in his post-non-apocalypse interviews he admitted to being shaken and "flabbergasted." It is certain that he convinced many others he was right. By employing his calculation-oriented method of biblical interpretation, he ensured an illusion that his date was logical and mathematical, and thus assured. As one of the disappointed disciples said to Tom Bartlett, "It all seemed so real, like it made so much sense."

MAYA LONG COUNT CALENDAR

WHAT WAS IT?

The Maya were a Mesoamerican civilization that flourished from the third through the tenth centuries CE. They were known for (among other things) stunning art and architecture, advanced mathematical skill, and accurate astronomical tables. Like the Aztec after them, the Maya used these skills to create highly complicated dating systems. Recently, one feature of the Maya calendar—the Long Count system—has become part of a new prediction about the end of the world.

The Maya Long Count calendar is based on cycles, in which time "rolls over" at various points, much the way we think of an odometer rolling over in a car. The cycles were of different lengths (akin to months, years, etc.), and calendars in classical Maya civilization marked the passing of these cycles and projected more out into the future. One such cycle, pertinent to the current discussion, was the baktun. This cycle was a period of 144,000 days, or a little less than four hundred years. Thirteen baktun cycles, 5,600 years, composed a Great Cycle.

The "Long Count" part of the name refers to a unique feature of this calendar. As the baktun cycles passed and as they considered baktun to come, the Maya were able to mark the passing of the cycle. Using the odometer analogy again, it would be as if, when the odometer on your car rolled back to zero, you drew a little hash mark on your dashboard. The numbers would reset, but you could also keep track of how many times they had. In much the same way, the Long Count calendar offers a way of keeping a constant chronology along-side the cyclical one. Long Count calendars with such methods of counting cycles are found throughout the area formerly occupied by the Maya people. In fact, recently a glyph was discovered in Guatemala that counts these cycles out seven thousand years into the future. (See http://news.nationalgeo graphic.com/news/2012/05/120510-maya-2012-doomsday-calendar-end-of-world-science?source=link_fb05102012 saturnomuralmaya&fb_source=message)

Based on Maya creation mythology, and correlating discussions of it to the Western calendar, the previous Great Cycle appears to have begun on August 11, 3114 BCE. Thus, the next turning of the odometer would occur on or about December 21, 2012.

Obviously, the Maya did not get their understanding of time from Judeo-Christian apocalyptic literature. And, by all accounts, the Maya who created the Long Count calendars did not in any way intend to indicate a catastrophic end of the world in 2012 by their marking of time. As Penn State professors Matthew Restall and Amara Solari put it so beautifully, "It is Western—not Maya—civilization that contains what we call the millenarian mother lode" (3). It is an indicator of the continuing power of apocalyptic worldview in our time that this ancient calendric system has caused a modern-day fervor in the West.

A quick Internet search reveals hundreds of books, movies, articles, and websites devoted to the supposed Maya Apocalypse. Many of these offer "explanations" of the ultimate meaning of the Long Count calendar, and they tend to fall into two categories: global devastation or global renewal. The first type of explanation often relies on combining the date with apocalyptic imagery drawn from biblical texts like Daniel and Revelation; the second depends more heavily on a New Age philosophical position. Since this book focuses on Judeo-Christian apocalyptic tradition and its outgrowths, we will focus on the first type. From this "devastation" camp, we will look at the writings and videos of John Claeys as just one example. His work is not representative of all 2012 apocalypticists, but he does offer a very interesting look at the methods used to combine two very different worldviews.

John Claeys is the author of the provocatively titled *Apocalypse 2012: The Ticking of the End Time Clock—What does the Bible say?* Aside from spectacular abilities in the use of punctuation, what the title clearly demonstrates is that the author is convinced the 2012 date is somehow related to biblical apocalypticism. While in the first chapter Claeys claims he is not setting a date for the prediction, throughout the book and on his (now-defunct) website, Claeys continuously asserts that cataclysmic events as described in Revelation might literally play out in 2012 ("or sooner!"), the year of the Maya cyclical reset. He describes the apocalyptic year will include sudden destructions, tribulation, and the ultimate overthrow of the world. Claeys is a premillennial dispensationalist and Christian Zionist, and his book owes more to Hal Lindsey than to the Maya Long Count calendar.

By way of explanation as to why 2012 is so significant to both Maya and Western apocalyptic calendars, Claeys stated thus on his website:

It seems the Mayans are also members of the borrowing-from-Christianity club. [T]he Mayan prediction regarding December 21, 2012 is another example of borrowing from Biblical Christianity. How do we know? First, the similarities regarding the returns of Bolon Yokte [a Mayan god of creation and war] and Jesus Christ align too closely to be coincidental. Second, the predictions regarding the return of Christ predate the Mayan prediction by nearly 700 years (New Testament) up to nearly 1,400 years (Isaiah). This clearly means that the borrowing was not that of the Bible from the Mayan inscription but of the Mayan recording from the Biblical accounts. (http://johnclaeys.com/the-mayan-prediction-of-2012-the-return-of-christ/)

Throughout this book, I have made it a point to believe the best about apocalypticists and their predictions, but saying that the Maya stole the idea of an apocalypse from Christianity simply strains believability to the point of breaking. It makes no sense in terms of how we understand the spread of cultures or ideas, nor does it coincide with what archaeologists and anthropologists know about Maya belief and cosmology. The claim—that Maya stole biblical concepts—is simply without merit or logic.

However "inexact" his comparison, Claeys' writings, as well as writings of some other apocalypticists, reflect a common conflation between biblical and non-biblical sources. (With only the most basic web search, one can find similar ideas on sites like christianityoasis.com and escapeallthesethings.com.) What happens in Claeys' work, and many other places, indicates the extent to which biblical apocalypticism has spread through modern consciousness. In the most sympathetic reading of the book above, we can say that Claeys is attempting to clarify that, in his thinking, biblical images of apocalypse supersede even material written by people who never encountered the Bible. Because he is so drawn to and grounded in images taken from Daniel, Thessalonians, and Revelation, any new (to him) description of the end times must somehow fit the biblical model.

WHAT WERE THE CONSEQUENCES OF THE FAILURE?

December 21, 2012, has not passed as of the completion of this book (although it will have by the time you read it!). So, I can't say for sure what the consequences of yet another failed apocalyptic prediction will be. I confess I feel pretty certain that this date will pass into history much like the others in this book. In truth, of course, the Long Count calendar date of December 21 is not a prediction of the apocalypse at all. But its use by Western non-indigenous people, particularly among fundamentalist Christian groups, does remind us that the apocalyptic worldview—which originated hundreds of years before, and half a world away—continues to exert an incredible pull on the modern imagination. In the final section of this book, I will consider why.

PART 3

WHEN THE WORLD DOESN'T END

★

While reading this book, how many times have you asked yourself, "They believed what?" or "How could those people think that?" We tend to approach apocalyptic groups by distancing ourselves from them, calling them crazy, or imagining them as weak personalities "brainwashed" by charismatic leaders. However, apocalyptic movements—no matter how often they fail—continue to draw new believers, and those believers are not so different from you or me in terms of their fears and hopes for a better future. But why, when the world never ends, are we still drawn to end-of-the-world ideas?

J. Z. Smith, author of *From Babylon to Jonestown*, has said on the subject of the Jonestown massacre, "If we do not persist in the quest for intelligibility [of the People's Temple movement], there can be no human sciences, let alone, any place for the study of religion within them" (120). That is, understanding religion and belief is about trying to find the sense of it, even in the most extreme cases, and even if the logic is purely internal to the group. If we are unable to do that, we miss out on making sense of how others see and make sense of the world. We alienate ourselves from our fellow human beings. Understanding is only a first step, of course. Once we can put ourselves in the shoes of another we can also take steps to prevent tragedies (whether of faith or of physical harm) because we can more successfully predict their occurrence.

In this section, then, I hope to offer a few conclusions that might help us better understand the people and ideas we have discussed here. First, I wish to consider what, if anything, we can say about apocalyptic movements through the ages. That is, what makes apocalyptic groups different than other religious organizations? What are some features that we could, to borrow a skill from the movements themselves, use to predict apocalyptic movements to come? Hopefully, our predictions will be a bit more accurate on the whole. Second, I wish to think a bit more on what draws people into, and keeps them coming back to, apocalypticism. Why, when the world doesn't end, do some among us inevitably latch on to the next date and time? And third, in the final section of the book, I wish to use some of what we learned to offer a few suggestions as to how we all might have a healthier attitude toward the end of the world.

FEATURES THAT REAPPEAR IN APOCALYPTICISM THROUGH THE AGES

When we first began to talk about apocalypticism as a Hellenistic Jewish alternative to wisdom, we saw several attributes that marked the worldview: a perception of persecution, a cosmological orientation, a desire for justice, a wish to know just how long until the faithful would be rewarded, etc. These community concerns were then evident in the texts we call apocalyptic: Enoch, Daniel, Thessalonians, Mark, and Revelation, just to name a few. With the closing of the Canon, the role of these texts changed somewhat, as they became sources of inspiration for the millennial movements that followed. We have seen the ways the language, ideas, and expectations of these ancient texts filled the many groups we studied. These texts continued to be living documents in the worlds of later believers, shaping their beliefs and contributing to their apocalyptic expectations.

However, the interpretation and reinterpretation of text to meet the current circumstance was not the only feature that marked apocalypticism after the biblical texts were written and accepted by the church. Over and over, we saw that millennial movements after the writing of Revelation featured the following: (1) charismatic leadership; (2) a belief that the current age must be the last age; (3) a desire among followers for order, consistency, rationality, or comprehensiveness in the universe; and (4) an overriding optimism about the future. This last feature might be the most debatable but I would argue that apocalyptic movements are overwhelmingly hopeful—perhaps not about the world in its current state, but at least about the potential for a better world to come.

CHARISMATIC LEADERSHIP

Charismatic leaders are individuals who, by the use of emotional connection (charm, manipulation, etc.), communication style, and/or relational power are able to convince others of the validity of their ideas or mission. Charismatic religious leaders are often seen by followers as uniquely gifted with the power of the divine (charisma) to lead those around them. Usually, these religious figures stand outside of conventional hierarchies and/or advocate for a radically different understanding of a religion, often creating conflict with the religious establishment. It is clear that most of the leaders we've identified with various apocalyptic movements were or are charismatic.

Scholars have attempted to understand why charismatic leaders are successful and gain such loyal followers, even in situations where such loyalty defies conventional standards. Max Weber, a sociologist of religion, indicated that charismatic leadership depends on both the internal qualities of the leader ("gifts") as well as the acceptance of the group (external acknowledgement). When groups accept charismatic leaders they are completely investing themselves in another person because of a deep need to overcome the constraints of their conventional world. The followers are in situations of crisis or distress, whether internal or external, and feel a loss of power that threatens their sense of self (Weber 245). Charismatic leaders appear to have the ability to manage such a crisis, allowing them to gain authority in the life of the believer. Identification with someone who seems able to overcome the same chaos that has so traumatized the believer is a powerful motivator.

Lorne Dawson, following up on the work of Weber but relating it specifically to millennial movements, agrees that charisma is often as dependent on the development of group feeling among the followers as any inherent qualities of the leaders. He expands Weber's discussion of the relational aspect of charisma, citing a long list of things that will likely result in a community believing that someone is a charismatic leader. Not all of these are necessary, but they are common. For example: the leader's actions are described as a model for the community; the leader's image or personality is displayed and referenced; the group itself is authoritarian in nature; the follower is repeatedly exposed to "internal folklore" or mythology that actively promotes the work of the leader; dissent is limited or eliminated; and so on. All of these reasons for the perception of charisma stem from the community rather than any innate "gifts" on the part of the leader. Dawson notes that, to outsiders, a charismatic leader may appear to be nothing of the sort. It is only when properly cultivated by the faithful that true charisma appears. Dawson's contribution here is significant because it reminds us that charisma is something that is created in community, over time; without buy-in from the followers, success or existence of charismatic leaders would be unlikely.

We have seen the importance of charismatic leadership and the investment of followers for continuing and expanding an apocalyptic movement. Unfortunately, the loyalty and invest-ment of followers in a charismatic leader can sometimes have disastrous spiritual or even life-threatening consequences. Reverend Jim Jones and the mass suicide of Peoples Temple members at Jonestown is perhaps the most famous example of this shadow side of charisma. Jones inspired great loyalty in his followers based in part on his personal appeal and com-munication style, but also because the values of racial har-mony and a coming age of reconciliation spoke meaningfully to the membership in a time of racial and civil unrest in the United States (Maaga xi). However, as outsiders "threatened" Jones it became more and more important to eliminate dis-sent and increase authoritarian structures, as well as separate the followers from the larger community. Catherine Wessinger reminds us that while charisma does not necessarily lead to the type of violence that occurred at Jonestown, moves to isolate and restrict access to the outside are more likely to lead to cat-astrophic consequences than a more open model of charisma.

EGOCENTRISM AND IMMEDIACY

A colleague of mine is fond of saying about apocalyptic pre-dictions, "No one ever predicts the apocalypse will come in ten thousand years." He's on to something, and we've seen it in the millennial movements in this book. With the exception of Pope Innocent III (who died shortly after he made his prediction), all of the prophets in this book saw the signs of the apocalypse pointing toward a date for the end of the world in their life-times. Honestly, this seems rather odd at first glance. After all, predicting the end much further out than you will live offers a sort of protection—a buffer—from having to deal with the failure if you are wrong.

And yet, we saw repeatedly that the date of the end corresponded closely with the span of the life of the predictor. This observation is confirmed in a landmark study conducted by psychoanalyst Charles Strozier, who interviewed apocalyptic believers in New York in the late 1980s and early 90s, all from the evangelical Christian tradition. One of the key findings of this study was that few if any of the apocalyptic faithful saw the world existing much beyond the range of their own lifetimes. Some were willing to extend the life of the world as far as a generation or two beyond theirs, but many, especially among working-class believers, tied the time of the apocalypse directly to the span of their own lives. For these apocalypticists at least, the frame of their lives was the frame of the life of the world.

It appears that, for at least a couple of reasons, humans are built to be egocentric in their apocalyptic thought. One reason is the consistent belief of human beings that they live in exceptional times. Psychologist Nicholas Christenfeld, in an interview for *Scientific American* discussing the Harold Camping predictions, described it this way: "It's part of the fundamental limited perspective of our species to believe that this moment is the critical one and critical in every way—for good, for bad, for the final end of humanity" (See http://www.scientific american.com/article.cfm?id=eternal-fascinations). That is, we tend to believe that this moment in world history is somehow

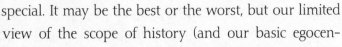

special. It may be the best or the worst, but our limited view of the scope of history (and our basic egocentrism) encourages us to believe that there will never be another moment like this one. Thus, it makes sense to us to think that this is the moment that the end of human history must occur.

In addition, we tend to view contemporary world events with a bit of fear that things could not possibly get worse. Each new problem seems bigger than the last, and each "enemy" the most formidable in history. This, of course, has been a feature of the apocalyptic worldview since its beginnings; it is why the phrase "How long, O Lord?" or some variation of it pops up again and again in the ancient texts we studied. But this long history of fear doesn't make today's fears any less scary. Whether the advancing Mongols or the threat of bank failure, we see the dangers of our own lifetime as the worst possible dangers of all. When combined with our general tendency to see our time on the planet as special, what results is a sense of an extremely ripe and tenuous present moment. In an interview with Stephanie Pappas of *LiveScience*, apocalyptic scholar Lorenzo DiTommaso concluded, "Problems have become so big, with no solutions in sight, that we no longer see ourselves able as human beings to solve these problems, [. . .] From a biblical point of view, God is going to solve them. From other points of view, there has to be some sort of catastrophe" (See http://www.livescience.com/14179-doomsday-psychology-21 -judgment-day-apocalypse.html). Either way, the great big-ness of the problems of our current world lead us to believe that the end must be coming, and it must be near—that is, soon.

CHAOS AVOIDANCE AND "RATIONALITY"

Another feature we have seen repeatedly in apocalyptic movements is the desire to have an orderly world, with an apparently rational progression from beginning to middle to end. Like most people, apocalypticists are troubled by the encroachment of chaos in their existence. But, unlike most people, the millennial imagination concludes that it can pinpoint—to the day sometimes—future events that will confirm that the present disorder is actually a temporary crisis.

We have discussed the fear that accompanies each age, as the world seems (to the believer) poised on the edge of total disorder. Thus, it should not surprise us that many of our prophets appealed to rationality or ordered thinking to express their apocalyptic "proof." Harold Camping and his mathematical gymnastics and Hal Lindsey (nicknamed "Mr. Logic" on the evangelical lecture circuit) come immediately to mind. Both relied on a sort of internal logic and appealed to a kind of rationality that provided structure to their arguments—and to their world. In *Arguing the Apocalypse*, Stephen O'Leary makes clear that apocalyptic predictions are not random or pointless. Rather, they function to offer a logical progression of ideas leading to an inevitable conclusion. He argues it is incredibly important to apocalyptic interpreters to make what they consider a "'logical' argument" based on the Bible (15). That is, apocalyptic rhetoric (way of speaking) among believers, and especially leaders, is specifically designed to make sense of a world in chaos by applying order, rationality, and logic (of a kind) to it. The resulting predictions, then, attempt to make sense of the disorder of the current world.

The ultimate chaos avoidance that millennialism seeks to address is the chaos of death. Obviously, no one is exempt from at least a twinge of fear about what comes after this life ends. This kind of fear is personal, as opposed to cosmological. It catches a person's breath in his or her chest. What apocalyptic prophecies do well is offer assurance and comfort in the midst of such shock and fear. We saw many such apocalyptic sects who offered assurance that death was not the end. The most extreme of these, perhaps, were the Heaven's Gate and Jonestown communities, but the desire to control death in other (non-fatal) cults is no less strong. Wessinger concludes her book with an assurance that the desire for an understanding of death means that apocalyptic cults will never disappear, but will always exist to reflect our human desire to overcome our finitude (284). That is, as long as humans fear the unknown frontier of death, there will be apocalyptic prophets offering solutions.

HOPE AND OPTIMISM

I would suggest that hope—and not ultimately pessimism—is the final feature that marks post-biblical apocalyptic movements. It may be misguided hope, and obviously being optimistic about the future world is not the same as working for good in the present. The "optimism" of apocalypticism can even lead to violence. However, it would be a disservice to understanding the nature of apocalypticism, and to understanding our fellow humans, to immediately demonize those who find meaning in apocalypticism as hopeless, fatalistic, pessimistic, violent zealots.

The optimism in apocalypticism comes from the consistent belief that something better is to come. It might require a radical break from the present world, even to the point of abandoning one's body, but there is a "light at the end of the tunnel." Apocalypticism, even in the ancient period, was marked by this sense of something better on the horizon. To be so, it relied on two concepts we generally associate with Western religions: linear time and divine justice. Unlike Eastern religions, Western faiths (Judaism, Christianity, and Islam) tend to view time as a line with a discernable beginning, middle, and end. Humans, too, are viewed as linear beings, whose lives begin, are lived, and inevitably end, never to be repeated. Obviously, this linearity lends itself to apocalypticism and judgment generally. But it also lends itself to an idea of the world as moving forward, progressing, toward something. Even if things seem bad in the present—even if they seem really bad—there is forward movement toward an inevitable end-goal, for humans individually and for the world as a whole.

It is not to be ignored that the Western religions are all monotheistic. This means they believe in one personal god who exercises control over the universe. Whereas in Eastern religions (like Hinduism and Buddhism) there is a sense that universal laws (like karma) govern the universe, in the Western faiths there is something (God) that stands outside the universe and could, at any point, intervene on behalf of the faithful. Apocalypticism, even at its most dire, affirms that this God will intervene eventually, will balance the scales of justice, and will appear to set things right. There is certainly a draw to such a worldview, especially for those who feel persecuted and wish for the problems in the current situation to be corrected. But just because it often results in predictions of the end of this world, that does not mean that the idea of a God who sets things right is not basically an optimistic notion.

Each of these features (charismatic leadership, egocentrism, chaos avoidance, and optimism) have appeared repeatedly in our discussion. While not every prediction we mentioned had all these elements, it is safe to say that these are characteristics we could expect to see if (or more likely when) someone predicts the world's demise yet again.

★ WHAT HAPPENED? THE MOST COMMON STRAT-EGIES FOR DEALING WITH FAILURE

Throughout this book, we asked, *What were the consequences of the failure?* We have seen instances where followers simply leave a movement quietly and go about their lives, but we have also seen instances where the consequences of a failed prophecy have been drastic or even fatal. If we are to learn anything from these situations we have to ask, *When the next "end of the world" is imagined, and when it fails, how will people cope?*

In the past, more often than not, people just carried on. Somehow, the participants took what they had experienced in their months or years prior and went about the business of living, even if they were sorely disappointed or financially ruined. What helped them cope with the failure? In the past fifty years, many social scientists have attempted to figure out how true believers manage to cope after failed apocalyptic predictions.

COGNITIVE DISSONANCE AND PROSELYTIZATION

Leon Festinger wrote perhaps the classic work on apocalyptic disappointments, *When Prophecy Fails.* Festinger was a social psychologist who was intrigued by the Millerites of the 1840s but had obviously been unable to study their behavior after the Great Disappointment firsthand. He was particularly interested in learning why so many of the most vehement of Miller's supporters continued to believe after the first failed prediction (in early 1844) and why many more continued to trust in the apocalypse after the Great Disappointment itself. Why had believers not abandoned the movement (and many like it) entirely, but pressed on in the face of overwhelming disconfirming evidence? Then, in 1954, Festinger was presented with a unique opportunity: to observe, firsthand, what happens when deeply held beliefs like those in the end of the world are disconfirmed.

In that year, Festinger and his associates learned about an apocalyptic UFO group begun by a woman in the Midwest. She had reported receiving telepathic messages of the apocalypse from the planet Clarion, which confirmed that the end would occur on December 21, 1954, by means of a flood that would destroy much of the earth. According to Festinger, the woman (given the pseudonym Dorothy Martin in *When Prophecy Fails* but whose real name was Marian Keech) attracted a small but devoted group of followers who sold their possessions and left behind their family connections to prepare for the apocalypse. These followers were known as "Seekers." Their hope was to avoid the coming flood by means of UFO transportation, which would arrive immediately before the cataclysmic event. Festinger and two associates infiltrated the group, posing as true believers, and documented the behavior and attitudes of group members when the expected end did not arrive.

Over the course of that November and December, the researchers watched as the membership of Seekers performed increasingly complex mental contortions to keep the disconfirming evidence in line with their beliefs. The researchers determined that, if certain conditions were met in an apocalyptic sect, failure of some aspects of a belief would in fact reconfirm the prevailing conviction. If predictions were specific (for example, involving a set date), if believers had sufficiently committed themselves to the movement (by leaving their families, for instance), and if they had found support in the group, believers were unlikely to immediately disband in the wake of an apocalyptic failure. However, to do so, the cognitive dissonance of the failed prophecy would first have to be managed.

"Cognitive dissonance" was Festinger's term for the mental disturbance that occurs when the beliefs one holds do not correspond with reality. For people like the Seekers, cognitive dissonance happened in the moments when the predictions of Dorothy Martin failed and the expected UFO did not arrive. However, because believers are so invested in their beliefs—in this case, to the point of abandoning their homes and possessions—they will go out of their way to justify and continue to hold the belief that appears to be at risk. Indeed, Festinger noted that even in the first hours after the failure, while still gathered in the place they had expected their deliverance to occur, believers were already resetting expectations and reorienting their prophetic ideals to fit the new reality.

However, reinterpretation was never enough, according to Festinger. To manage the cognitive dissonance, true believers had to go still further, redoubling efforts to convince others of the rightness of their convictions. Festinger concluded that the effort to convince others is the most effective way of dealing with the mental frustration of a failed belief. There is, according to Festinger, a critical mass of people necessary to support struggling belief and to battle contradictory evidence. Festinger noted that explanation and openness among believers often follow a failed prediction, whether in the media or toward the populace at large. The hope is to cement one's own belief by drawing others into it. If enough people agree with a believer, it must be right.

Festinger's theory gives us a useful piece of the puzzle for understanding why apocalypticism continues even when apocalyptic predictions fail. Festinger notes the importance of the individual members' shared beliefs in dealing with an apocalyptic failure. One of the surest ways to keep an apocalyptic movement or belief system alive is to convince more people that it is so; believers reconfirm their own faith by telling themselves that if others believe it they can continue to trust the idea as well. We encountered this repeatedly throughout this book: the Millerites (the sect that first piqued Festinger's interest) redoubled their efforts and launched the Seventh-Day Adventist movement, which in turn spawned the Davidians; the Jehovah's Witnesses sought even more converts after 1975; the True Way held a press conference to celebrate the "success" of their failed apocalypse in 1998. In each case, believers used failed predictions to shore up the hearts of the faithful and to appeal to the minds of potential new converts.

Assurance of the fundamental "truth" of apocalyptic belief often relies on the assurances of the leader, and I would offer this as a sort of subset of the Festinger hypothesis on proselytization. Millenarian movements are often dependent on strong, seemingly inspired leaders: Bar Koziba, Montanus, Hans Hut, Jim Jones, David Koresh, Harold Camping. The quick response of a charismatic leader to a failure, especially to affirm the basic accuracy of the worldview and the faithfulness of the believers in question, can often be the difference between a continued or abandoned sect.

> A sect is a smaller group within a religious tradition. The beliefs of the sect are usually distinctive when compared to the "parent" religion, and often set them at odds with the larger tradition.

Susan Palmer and Natalie Finn agree, noting that a prophet's skill in reinventing a belief system after a failed prediction is often a critical factor in changing the perception among followers from a sense of failure to a sense of success (399). This is not to suggest that a movement might not find success without the assurances of a charismatic figure; in the case of the Millerites, for example, William Miller played no role in the development of Adventism post-1844. However, the assurance that a role model so thoroughly continues to trust in her/his predictions, in spite of disconfirmation, can lessen the cognitive dissonance and allow apocalyptic hope to continue.

RATIONALIZATION AND REAFFIRMATION

When Prophecy Fails provides a starting point for understanding why people continue to believe after a prophetic failure, but it cannot account for all of the movements we studied. For example, most of the movements did not increase proselytization after a failure, a fact which subsequent scholars of apocalyptic religions didn't fail to notice. (In one review of cases, conducted by Lorne Dawson, it was determined that only a small number of studied groups actually increased proselytization [60–61].) Some scholars disputed the entire theory of cognitive dissonance and proselytization as a way to understand apocalyptic belief after failures; most, however, suggested that a single answer to the question at hand was impossible and that multiple features must be taken into account.

Lorne Dawson, a sociologist of religion, has noted two additional strategies for dealing with failure: rationalization and reaffirmation.

Rationalization is the process of reinterpreting the current facts (post-failure) until they match the worldview of the believer. Reaffirmation is the continued reassertion of the importance of the community, its structure, and its goals following the failure of an apocalyptic prediction.

The first strategy is rationalization, and it has four sub-strategies, which we can apply to many apocalyptic groups. Dawson's sub-strategies include:

- spiritualization
- a test of faith
- human error
- blaming others

Spiritualization rationalizes the seeming disconfirmation of the apocalypse by claiming that it has happened, but in another (spiritual) realm. Spiritualization affirms one basic idea of apocalyptic groups—that this world is part of a larger, cosmic realm—while also accounting for what seems to have been disproven to non-believers. The Millerites, Jehovah's Witnesses, the True Way, and Harold Camping clearly used this strategy to rationalize why there were no obvious world ending catastrophes. When the October 1844 apocalypse did not occur, Millerite followers claimed the very next day that the planned apocalypse had indeed arrived, but in spirit rather than on earth. The idea of a spiritual eschaton marks Seventh-Day Adventist tradition to this day. Similarly, the Jehovah's Witnesses affirmed that the 1914 apocalypse did indeed happen, and that they were presently living in the millennial reign of Christ. When the leader of the True Way met reporters, he spiritualized the claim that God would appear and shake the hand of everyone present by suggesting that God had been present in the spirit of each person there.

Dawson points to a second common rationalization: the failed apocalypse as a test of faith. In this rationalization, it is sometimes claimed that the faithful were able to delay the end by their conviction; alternately, the believers will claim that the failure is a means for God to test the strength of their convictions, especially in the midst of the inevitable public ridicule that follows failure.

The third type of rationalization is human error, the idea that somehow people misunderstood the divine message and need to recalculate. Harold Camping's earliest predictions, in the 1990s, led to this type of rationalization.

The final and more rare type of response, according to Dawson, is blaming others. In the case of the Jehovah's Witnesses, when nothing happened in 1975, the president of the Watch-tower Society placed blame squarely on the shoulders of the believers (68). It is slightly more common to blame outsiders (such as the "unfaithful" or the media), but this is unusual as well in the face of a failed prediction.

Dawson goes on to suggest that, while rationalization is important, reaffirmation is the most common way of follow-ers coping when a prophecy fails. In his review of the case studies, he noted that almost every group used this method of self-protection against dissonance (69). Reaffirmation is essen-tially validation of the community itself. When the date of the end passes, the members of a community rally themselves in order to continue the support and unity they have come to need. Sometimes, this results in a reorganization, as happened with the Millerites. It can involve a reinterpretation of the pur-pose of the group such as with the True Way group. Other times it results in a reimagining of the role or timing of the messiah, even at his peril, as the rabbis did post-Bar Kochba. The key aspect of reaffirmation is that it keeps intact the com-munity that has come to mean everything to the believers. Whatever the method, reaffirmation allows the faithful to keep the sense of purpose and family that the community provided. Given our basic human need for community, it is no surprise that reaffirmation is the hallmark of apocalyptic belief after a failed prediction.

The groups discussed also verify two more of Dawson's reasons for the continuation of apocalypticism when spe-cific predictions fail. First, the apocalyptic worldview is built for reinterpretation. The ability to reinterpret and incorporate facts that clearly disprove predictions (by spiritualization or blame, for example) is a characteristic of an apocalyptic prophet's thought process. The earliest apocalyptic texts were a response to the failure of wisdom traditions to account for a world where the righteous suffered while the wicked prospered. The gospel of Mark and Revelation are both reinterpretations of the apocalyptic visions in the book of Daniel. The failed movements we've seen are later calculations and reinterpretations of these same ancient texts. This is possible because the language of apocalyptic writing is so flexible. It is full of indirect language (like imagery and symbol) that readers can change to suit their own circumstance, and fill with meaning from their own experiences (see Thatcher 550).

A SINGLE IMAGE CAN HAVE MULTIPLE MEANINGS IN MULTIPLE CONTEXTS, AND STILL BE MEANINGFUL, AS LONG AS THE BELIEVER INVESTS HER- OR HIMSELF IN THE CREATION OF THAT MEANING.

Apocalyptic writers did not present material in terms of facts and concrete objects. Instead these writers used images and metaphor. It is those symbols and metaphors that make it possible for a person to apply the texts to events in his or her own time. If the mark of the beast turns out not to be Roman Imperial power, for example, then perhaps it was Turks in the Holy Land or American ATF agents.

In this way, many of the apocalyptic prophets and movements throughout history were able to predict the end of the world again and again, sometimes within hours of the failure of the first, without feeling they really failed at all.

The movements we have seen show that apocalyptic belief succeeds because believers value the community they find with fellow members, another of Dawson's reasons why apocalyptic movements continue after a prediction fails. Such community—especially in cases where believers abandon family, friends, work, school, and other routines—becomes the entire world of the faithful. Abandoning the apocalyptic beliefs would mean abandoning the believers, and such an act would cause psychological harm to the most invested members of the community. It is obvious, then, that apocalyptic beliefs would continue in these intensive, separatist groups, in spite of failed prophecy. But even among the less intensely invested believers, the role of community is significant. Ever since the work of sociologist Emile Durkheim, people who study how society influences individual behavior have known that one of the functions of religion is to provide structure to the lives of individuals and the transmission of worldviews from one generation to the next. The communal function of religion that gives moral guidance and promotes a sense of cooperation is clearly evidenced in the many religious groups we encountered. Even on occasions when we might have questioned those communities or their ideals, we must agree that no apocalyptic prediction occurred without a supporting community; all came from and were nurtured by a group of people, even when a strong charismatic leader was present.

FUTURE HOPE AND ESCAPE

The work we've seen done by the sociologists and psychologists studying millennial groups emphasizes what can be known from observing human behavior. These studies are critically important and offer us key insight into the nature of apocalyptic movements. However, from the perspective of a believer within one of these groups, it is unlikely that she or he would describe the experience of apocalyptic disappointment in the terms of cognitive dissonance and rationalization (however correct they might be). It is important to ask what his or her perspective is. We must ask what those people think their reasons are for coming back and for investing again and again in the apocalyptic movement.

Theologian Ulrich Kortner notes that the key feature that keeps religious people coming back to apocalyptic predictions is the real hope that there is an escape from a believer's feelings of persecution, sadness, or disorder, wherever they originate. He says that the hope in apocalyptic belief is like the discovery of a door (an "egress") that directs the person's actions and becomes both the source and the goal of hope when things seem futile or scary (207). To the apocalyptic believer, the draw of hope for an escape to a better world, a world redeemed by God and away from the concerns of this world, will always be preferable to the present reality.

This belief in future hope that these movements and others offer can be wonderful. There is something about apocalypticism that does appeal to our deeply rooted desire to see goodness and justice, and to believe—sometimes against odds—that there is hopefulness to be found somewhere. From a theological perspective, the hopefulness in apocalypticism can affirm that God is good and that evil will be conquered. However, this future hope can be fatalistic as well. It can make us look for an egress, as Kortner calls it, rather than seeking the good of this world and its people. We saw this type of extreme fatalism (and basic pessimism for any redemption of the current world) in the premillennialist beliefs of dispensationalists. And, as we saw with the people of Heaven's Gate, apocalyptic fatalism can even lead millennial believers to take their own lives in an effort to accelerate this path to egress.

CONCLUSION: IT'S THE END OF THE WORLD! OR MAYBE NOT?

The discussion within this book does not nearly begin to cover all of the many studies, theories, and theological ideas that attempt to explain why apocalyptic movements continue in the face of failures. I offer the ones above, however, because they not only touch on some of the reasons people continue to believe, but provide us a way to think about how we might approach the words of the next prophet to set a date for the end of the world.

Over the past few months, when people I met asked what I was writing, the conversation usually took a very predictable turn. I would describe the goals of the book: to introduce the reader to the history of apocalyptic thought from the earliest writers, to show how the seeds of apocalyptic ideas came to be a part of Western culture, and to offer reasons for why so many might believe when the failure rate for apocalyptic predictions sat right at 100 percent. A curious person would listen politely, and then (more often than not) reply with the same question: "How do you know they won't be right next time?"

I share this story because I think it points to the obvious and continuous draw of apocalyptic thought. As we have seen, we tend to view the span of the world as equivalent to our own life span; we tend to see the world as heading toward an inevitable conclusion because we have a linear outlook; and our minds have remarkable abilities to manage incompatible information while maintaining the capacity to reaffirm our basic mindset, even in the face of overwhelming evidence to the contrary. With all of these mental and spiritual processes at work, it is no surprise that no number of examples of failure could convince us that the next one wouldn't be—finally—the prediction that got it right.

As you contemplate the possibility of the end of the world, remember these things:

FIRST, DON'T CONFUSE CHARISMA WITH INFORMATION.

Yes, preaching and teaching can be powerful and can appeal to our spiritual selves in a way books and facts sometimes can't. But one of the features we saw over and over, especially in millennial groups that turned destructive, was the tendency to invest heavenly force into the words of the leader/prophet.

No person is divine, and all people are fallible. To trust a preacher or teacher to the point where you turn off your own brain is dangerous. Be especially wary of charismatic leaders who want you to abandon family, sever ties to the day-to-day world, and listen only to them. A variety of voices can help you weigh the claims of apocalyptic prophets, but you need to have access to these different ways of thinking. If someone truly believes he or she is right, that person will not fear your reading things that disagree or question.

As we have seen, apocalyptic predictions are almost always made for a date in the lifetime of the prophet. Why? Because we fail to remember that our lives do not make up the lifespan of the world, and we tend to see ourselves and our reality as somehow special. I am sorry if I am the first to tell you, but millions of people have come before you, and millions more will live here after you are gone. The universe is massive, and you are, after all, a very tiny speck compared to its vastness. It's humbling. I am not trying to depress anyone, but simply to protect us against the sort of rampaging self-centeredness that promotes recklessness.

Remembering our place in the universe, however, does not need to inspire fatalism either. When we consider that we are here right now, and that whatever is yet to come is unknown, we can be inspired to make this world the best it can be for the present moment. After all, if there is one thing we saw repeatedly from the failed apocalyptic predictions, it is that people can inspire others to massive changes in behavior by their words and ideas. What they have used to mislead (whether on purpose or by accident), we could use to create lasting change for the good. Perhaps in so doing we can stop the kind of apocalyptic events this book did not discuss: preventable threats such as climate change, destructive poverty, and economic injustices. Remembering our place in the universe balances humility for our smallness with our awe at our potential to produce change.

SECOND, BE AWARE OF YOUR PLACE IN THE UNIVERSE.

This book has shown you just a fraction of the guesses and goofs that have made up Western apocalyptic history, but these few examples do clearly bear out the very ancient insight from the gospel of Matthew. While thinking you can pinpoint the end of the world might, briefly, provide comfort and ease your feelings of chaos, it is (and has always been) a futile endeavor because—in the final analysis—no one can predict the future with absolute certainty.

Hopefully, in reading this book, you have come to understand a bit more of the mindset that leads to apocalypticism, why apocalyptic thought persists, and perhaps why some folks would be willing to sacrifice everything to believe that the next prediction of the end is the "real" one. I confess that in researching and writing this, my own perspective has been changed significantly; I have come to see the power, the optimism, and the intense draw of millennial thought, and to feel real empathy for those who are so fearful and feel so persecuted that they truly believe that the only answer is that this earthly torture will end, and that the end is at hand.

FINALLY, I OFFER SOME BIBLICAL WISDOM: "BUT ABOUT THAT DAY AND HOUR NO ONE KNOWS, NEITHER THE ANGELS OF HEAVEN, NOR THE SON, BUT ONLY THE FATHER" (MATT. 24:36).

I do not advocate a millennial mindset. Clearly some of these groups justify violence committed in the name of bringing the apocalypse, and that is unacceptable. Seeking understanding and feeling empathy does not mean that we approve of the mistreatment and self- or other-destruction many of these groups have encouraged. However, understanding and empathy can help us prevent such violence from occurring again. A carefully cultivated awareness of apocalyptic and millennial belief systems can make us more sensitive to the potential in some groups to turn violent. It is only with such awareness that we can then seek to stop potentially violent groups before things go awry. Obviously, empathy and understanding will also help us determine when a group of believers is not a threat to the safety of others.

In the process of writing this book, I got to do what J. Z. Smith suggested we all do: seek understanding, of even the most different kinds of religious persons, so that we can better appreciate what makes us all human. I hope perhaps it has helped you do the same.

BIBLIOGRAPHY

Bader, Chris. "When Prophecy Passes Unnoticed: New Perspectives on Failed Prophecy." *JSSR* 38.1 (1999): 119–31.

Barkun, Michael. *A Culture of Conspiracy: Apocalyptic Visions in Contemporary America.* Berkeley: University of California Press, 2006.

Bartlett, Tom. "A Year After the Non-Apocalypse: Where Are They Now?" religiondispatches.org. May 2012.

Boyer, Paul. *When Time Shall Be No More: Prophecy Belief in Modern American Culture.* Cambridge: Harvard University Press, 1992.

Brown, Ira V. "Watchers for the Second Coming: The Millenarian Tradition in America." *The Mississippi Valley Historical Review* 39.3 (1952): 441–58.

Butler, Jonathan. "From Millerism to Seventh-Day Adventism: 'Boundless to Consolidation.'" *Church History* 55.1 (1986): 50–64.

Camping, Harold. *Are You Ready?* familyradio.com

—. *We Are Almost There!* familyradio.com

Charlesworth, J. H., ed. *The Old Testament Pseudepigrapha Vols. 1–2.* Yale University Press, 1983.

Chidester, David. *Salvation and Suicide?: Jim Jones, the Peoples Temple, and Jonestown?.* Bloomington: Indiana University Press, 2003.

Claeys, John. *Apocalypse 2012: The Ticking of the End Time Clock.* Sisters, OR: VMI Publishers, 2010.

Clark, Kent. "The Problem of Pseudonymity in Biblical Literature and Its Implications for Canon Formation." In *The Canon Debate.*, edited by Lee Martin MacDonald and James A. Sanders, 440–68. Peabody, MA: Hendrickson, 2002.

Collins, J. *The Apocalyptic Imagination: An Introduction to Jewish Apocalyptic Literature.* 2nd ed. Grand Rapids: Eerdmans, 1998.

Cohn, Norman. *Cosmos, Chaos, & the World to Come: The Ancient Roots of Apocalyptic Faith*. Yale University Press, 2001.

Cowan, Douglas. "Confronting the Failed Failure: Y2K and Evangelical Eschatology in Light of the Passed Millennium." *Nova Religio* 7.2 (2003): 71–85.

Crompton, Robert. *Counting the Days to Armageddon: Jehovah's Witnesses and the Second Presence of Christ*. Cambridge: James Clark, 1996.

Culp, Bruce. "The Not-Very True Way: After the World Didn't End as Predicted, Teacher Chen and the Remnant of His Followers Still See Signs the Great Tribulation is Nigh." *The Ottawa Citizen*. January 2, 2000.

Cook, Stephen L. *Prophecy & Apocalypticism: The Postexilic Social Setting*. Minneapolis: Augsburg Fortress, 1995.

Dawson, Lorne L. "When Prophecy Fails and Faith Persists: A Theoretical Overview." *Nova Religio* 3.1 (1999): 60–82.

Drosnin, Michael. *The Bible Code*. New York: Touchstone, 1997.

Eck, Werner. "The Bar Kokhba Revolt: The Roman Point of View." *JRS 59* (1999): 78–89.

Ehrman, Bart. *The New Testament: A Historical Introduction to the Early Christian Writings. 5th ed*. Oxford: Oxford University Press, 2011.

Festinger, Leon, Riecken, Henry W., and Stanley Schachter. *When Prophecy Fails*. Minneapolis: University of Minnesota Press, 1956.

Frassetto, Michael, ed. *The Year 1000: Religious and Social Responses to the Turning of the First Millennium*. New York: Palgrave Macmillan, 2002.

Frykholm, Amy Johnson. *Rapture Culture*: Left Behind *in Evangelical America*. Oxford: Oxford University Press, 1004.

Goffard, Christopher. "Harold Camping Is at the Heart of a Mediapocalypse." *Los Angeles Times* May 21, 2011.

Grünschloß, Andreas. "When We Enter Into My Father's Spacecraft: Cargoistic Hopes and Millenarian Cosmologies in New Religious UFO Movements." http://wwwuser.gwdg.de/~agruens/UFO/ufocargo_final. html#FNT28. Accessed August 1, 2012.

Henton, J. "Dragon Myth and Imperial Ideology in Revelation 12–13." In *The Reality of Apocalypse: Rhetoric and Politics in the Book of Revelation*, edited by David L. Barr, ed. 181–201. Atlanta: SBL, 2006.

Himmelfarb, Martha. "Revelation and Rabbinization in Sefer Zerubbabel and Sefer Eliyyahu." In *Revelation, Literature and Community in Late Antiquity*, edited by Philippa Townsend and Moulie Vidas, 217–36. Tubingen: Mohr Siebeck, 2011.

Hoffman, G. "Why the Concern About Y2K?" *Etc: A Review of General Semantics* 57.1 (2000): 97.

Holden, Andrew. *Jehovah's Witnesses: Portrait of a Contemporary Religious Movement*. New York: Routledge, 2002.

Jacobs, Janet. "Deconversion from Religious Movements: An Analysis of Charismatic Bonding and Spiritual Commitment." *JSSR* 26.3 (1987): 294–308.

Johnson, Paul. *A History of Christianity*. New York: Atheneum, 1976.

Kliever, Lonnie D. "Meeting God in Garland: A Model of Religious Tolerance." *Nova Religio* 3.1 (1999): 45–53.

Kortner, Ulrich. *The End of the World: A Theological Interpretation*. Louisville: Westminster John Knox, 1988.

Krey, August C. *The First Crusade: The Accounts of Eyewitnesses and Participants*, Princeton: Princeton University Press, 1921.

Lawson, Ronald. "The Persistence of Apocalypticism Within a Denominationalizing Sect: The Apocalyptic Fringe Groups of Seventh-Day Adventists." In *Millennium, Messiahs, and Mayhem: Contemporary Apocalyptic Movements*, edited by Thomas Robbins and Susan Palmer, 207-28. New York: Routledge, 1997. 207–228.

Lee, Dan P. "After the Rapture." *New York* October 16, 2011.

Lindsey, Hal. *The Late Great Planet Earth*. Grand Rapids: Zondervan, 1970.

—. *The 1980s: Countdown to Armageddon.* New York: Bantam, 1981.

Lippy, Charles H. "Waiting for the End: The Social Context of American Apocalyptic Religion." In *The Apocalyptic Vision in America*, edited by Lois Zamora, 37–63. Bowling Green: Bowling Green University Popular Press, 1982.

Maaga, Mary McCormick. *Hearing the Voices of Jonestown: Putting a Human Face on an American Tragedy.* Syracuse: Syracuse University Press, 1998.

Mayer, Jean-Francois. "The Movement for the Restoration of the Ten Commandments of God." *Nova Religio* 5.1 (2001): 203–210.

McArthur, Benjamin. "Millennial Fevers." *Reviews in American History.* 24.3 (1996): 369–382.

McGinn, Bernard. *Visions of the End: Apocalyptic Traditions in the Middle Ages.* New York: Columbia University Press, 1979.

McMinn, Lisa. "Y2K, The Apocalypse, and Evangelical Christianity: The Role of Eschatological Belief in Church Responses." *Sociology of Religion.* 62.2 (2001): 205–220.

Metzger, Bruce M. "Literary Forgeries and Canonical Pseudepigrapha." *JBL* 91 (1972): 3–24.

Moyer, Michael. "Eternal Fascinations with the End: Why We're Suckers for Stories of Our Own Demise." *Scientific American* August 18, 2010.

Murphy, Francesca Aran. "Revelation (The Apocalypse of St. John the Divine): Revelation and Canon." In *Theological Interpretation of the New Testament.*, edited by Kevin Vanhoozer, 234–47. Grand Rapids: Baker, 2008.

Newman, Sharan. *The Real History of the End of the World.* New York: Berkley Books, 2010.

Newport, Kenneth G. C. *The Branch Davidians of Waco: The History and Beliefs of an Apocalyptic Sect.* Oxford: Oxford University Press, 2006.

O'Brien, Kathleen. "It's 2012, Another Year for Doomsday Chatter." *Christian Century* 129.3 (2012): 21.

O'Leary, Stephen. *Arguing the Apocalypse: A Theory of Millennial Rhetoric.* Oxford: Oxford University Press, 2008.

—. "When Prophecy Fails and When It Succeeds: Apocalyptic Prediction and Re-Entry into Ordinary Time." In *Apocalyptic Time.*, edited by Albert Bumgarten, 342–62. Leiden: Brill, 2000.

"No Show by God on Live TV." *The Daily Telegraph.* Sydney, Australia. March 26, 1998.

Packull, Werner O. "In Search of the 'Common Man' in Early German Anabaptist Ideology." *The Sixteenth Century Journal* 17.1 (1986): 51–67.

Palmer, Susan J. and Natalie Finn, "Coping with Apocalypse in Canada: Experiences of Endtime in *La Mission de l'Esprit Saint* and the Institute of Applied Metaphysics." *Sociological Analysis* 53 (1992): 397–415.

Penton, M. James. *Apocalypse Delayed: The Story of the Jehovah's Witnesses.* Toronto: University of Toronto Press, 2002.

Pippin, Tina. *Apocalyptic Bodies: The Biblical End of the World in Text and Image.* New York: Taylor and Francis, 1999.

Von Rad, Gerhard. *Old Testament Theology: The Theology of Israel's Traditions.* Louisville: Westminster John Knox, 2001.

Von Rad, Restall, Matthew and Amara Solari. *2012 and the End of the World: The Western Roots of the Maya Apocalypse.* Lanham, MD: Rowan and Littlefield, 2011.

Reeves, John. "Sefer Zerubbabel." *Trajectories in Near Eastern Apocalyptic.* Atlanta: SBL, 2005.

Rosen, Elizabeth K. *Apocalyptic Transformation: Apocalypse and the Postmodern Imagination.* Lanham, MD: Lexington Books, 2008.

Russell, D. S. *The Method and Message of Jewish Apocalyptic: 200 BC—AD 100.* Philadelphia: Westminster, 1964.

Schmithals, Walter. *The Apocalyptic Movement: Introduction and Interpretation.* John E. Steely, transl. Nashville: Abingdon, 1973.

Schussler-Fiorenza, Elisabeth. *Revelation: Vision of a Just World*. Minneapolis: Fortress, 1991.

Shermer, Michael. "The End is Always Nigh." *New Scientist* 210.2815 (2011): 30–31.

Singleberg, Richard. "'It Separated the Wheat from the Chaff': The "1975" Prophecy and Its Impact Among Dutch Jehovah's Witnesses." *Sociological Analysis* 50.1 (1989): 23–40.

Sitler, Robert K. "The 2012 Phenomenon New Age Appropriation of an Ancient Mayan Calendar." *Nova Religio* 9.3 (2006): 24–38.

Smith, J. Z. *Imagining Religion: From Babylon to Jonestown*. Chicago: University Chicago Press, 1982.

—. *Map Is Not Territory: Studies in the History of Religions*. Leiden: Brill, 1978.

Stark, Rodney. "Why Religious Movements Succeed or Fail: A Revised General Model." *JCR* 11.2 (1996): 133–46.

Stark, Rodney and William Sims Bainbridge. "Of Churches, Sects, and Cults: Preliminary Concerns for a Theory of Religious Movements." *JSSR* 18.2 (1979): 117–131.

Strozier, J. *Apocalypse: On the Psychology of Fundamentalism in America*. New York: Beacon: 1994.

Tapia, Andrea Hoplight. "Techno-Armageddon: The Millennial Christian Response to Y2K." *Review of Religious Research* 43.3 (2002): 266–286.

Taysom, Stephen. *Shakers, Mormons, and Religious Worlds: Conflicting Visions, Contested Boundaries*. Bloomington: Indiana University Press, 2011.

Thatcher, Tom. "Empty Metaphors and Apocalyptic Rhetoric." *JAAR* 66. 3 (1998): 549–570.

Thompson, Damian. *The End of Time: Faith and Fear in the Shadow of the Millennium*. Hanover: University Press of New England, 1996.

Tolan, John V. *Saracens: Islam in the Medieval European Imagination*. New York: Columbia University Press, 2002.

United States Senate Special Committee on the Year 2000 Technology Problem. *Y2K Aftermath—A Crisis Averted.* 2000. senate.gov.

Vance, Erik. "Mayan Calendar: World Will Not End In December 2012, Expert Says." *Scientific American* July 8, 2012.

Wallis, John. "Making Sense of the Movement for the Restoration of the Ten Commandments of God." *Nova Religio 9* (2005): 49–66.

—. *Wisdom in Israel.* Harrisburg, PA: Trinity Press International, 1972.

Weddle, David. "A New 'Generation' of Jehovah's Witnesses: Revised Interpretation, Ritual, and Identity." *Nova Religio* 3.2 (2000): 350–67.

Wessinger, Catherine. *How the Millennium Comes Violently: From Jonestown to Heaven's Gate.* New York: Seven Bridges, 2000.

Wojcik, Daniel. "Embracing Doomsday: Faith, Fatalism, and Apocalyptic Belief in the Nuclear Age." *Western Folklore* 55.4 (1996): 297–330.

—. *The End of the World as We Know It: Faith, Fatalism, and Apocalypse in America.* New York: New York University Press, 1997.

Yadin, Yigael. *Bar-Kokhba?: The Rediscovery of the Legendary Hero of the Second Jewish Revolt Against Rome.* New York: Random House, 1971.

Zamora, Lois Parkinson, ed. *The Apocalyptic Vision in America.* Bowling Green: Bowling Green University Popular Press, 1982.